CASTLES
OF
DEVON
James Mildren

BOSSINEY BOOKS

First published in 1987
by Bossiney Books
St Teath, Bodmin, Cornwall.

Designed, printed and bound in
Great Britain by Penwell Ltd,
Parkwood, Callington, Cornwall.

PLATE ACKNOWLEDGMENTS
Front cover by Roy Westlake
Julian Mildren: Pages 7, 8, 11, 16,
    19, 23, 27, 31, 36, 41, 44, 47,
    49, 54, 59, 61, 65, 74, 76, 79,
    83, 84, 86 and back cover
Stephen Mildren: Pages 12, 21,
    24, 33, 43, 53, 70, 88
Paul Honeywill: Page 35
By courtesy of The National
    Trust: Pages 9, 12, 15, 20, 23,
    33, 43, 53, 70, 88
By courtesy of *The Western
    Morning News*: Page 40

Contents

About the Author—and the Book

James Mildren, well-known Westcountry journalist, completes a Bossiney hat-trick for the Cornish cottage publishers of St Teath. He has worked for *The Western Morning News* since 1967, and his two previous publications for Bossiney are *Dartmoor in the Old Days*, published in 1984 and still in print, and *125 Years with The Western Morning News*.

Here in the company of his sons, Julian and Stephen, he tours the *Castles of Devon*. Castle Drogo, Lydford, Gidleigh, Okehampton, Barnstaple and Watermouth are only some of the castles featured.

The author reflects: 'The castles of Devon are a valuable, loved and wholly delightful portion of our heritage, whether they are a pile of ruins or some still developing entity. They offer a unique educational opportunity, and a rich and fulfilling visual experience. As a test of history and imagination, they are unique, and intensely human in their appeal.'

Nearly all the photographs and all the drawings have been especially commissioned for this, Bossiney's 141st title.

Julian Mildren, who took most of the photographs was born in Devonport, and now lives in Tavistock, where he was educated. Stephen Mildren, the book's illustrator, was born in Tavistock. He is married and now lives in Cardiff. He was awarded his BA (Hons) in Graphic Design at Newport and his MA at Manchester in 1985.

Right: The author, James Mildren.

Castles of Devon

The castles of Devon are eloquent, meaningful reminders of the restless spirit of our ancestors. Few buildings in the county are more human in their appeal or so rich in historical association.

The Normans begat them to consolidate, by force of arms if necessary, the manorial possessions of a handful of powerful noblemen to whom a grateful but determined Conqueror had doled out vast acreages of land. The Normans were plain, practical men. No fairy-tale edifice rose like some peregrine's eyrie floating and shimmering high above a Devon valley. No ludicrous Bavarian pile. Bogus-gothic turrets and towers were to come much later in time.

A place showeth the man—and it showeth some to the better and some to the worse, wrote Bacon.

The Norman success in the west lay in the possession of its largest community—Exeter. The Romans before them realised that simple fact. William the Conqueror set about suppressing the city some eighteen months after his victory at Hastings: he understood not only the inherent rebellious nature of the western people, but the danger on that flank from Harold's avenging sons.

He secured his domination by establishing the great Rougemont Castle, and ensuring that his liegemen created similar defences at Okehampton and Totnes, Barnstaple and Plympton.

In just two decades, between 1066 and 1086, practically every-thing worthwhile in Devon had undergone a change in ownership. A handful of William's followers wielded sovereign power—Baldwin de Brionne (sheriff), Judhael of Totnes (later Barnstaple), the de Pomeroys, the Bishop of Coutances and the Capra family. Lesser

Right: The gardens at Castle Drogo almost 1,000 feet up on Dartmoor.

Normans also infiltrated the county creating smaller castles at such places as Blackwell Rings, Loddiswell, and at Winkleigh and Chumleigh. These disappeared long ago. But there were others which deserve further consideration—at Hemyock, for example, built in 1380 by William de Asthorp a Northamptonshire knight, who had the temerity, like the Bonvilles, to challenge the mighty Courtenay family. There were castles, also, at Salcombe (Tudor, or even older), at Great Torrington and Bampton, Holwell (Parracombe), Heywood (Wembworthy), Durpley (Shebbear) and Burley Wood (Bridestowe).

This little book, and it is in no way an exhaustive account, examines some of the obvious survivals in the Devon landscape. In addition to Rougemont, Okehampton, Totnes, Barnstaple and Plympton, it looks at Tiverton (1106), Bickleigh (1110), Lydford (1195), Plymouth (1220), Gidleigh (1300), Berry Pomeroy (1300), Compton (1340), Powderham (1390), Dartmouth (1481) and

Left: Crenellated Powderham. Below: Julius Drewe, who commissioned Lutyens to create Castle Drogo.

Kingswear (1491): the dating can be approximate only. Watermouth (1826) and Drogo (1911) are historic upstarts in such company, lovely though they are.

However, it is not my intention to be drawn into any learned discussion on what, precisely, comprises a castle.

The popular conception that an Englishman's house, or home, is his castle was first expressed, it appears, by an Elizabethan, Sir Edward Coke (1552-1634). But the first mention of the word castle in English records appears in 1048, when King Edward the Confessor visited such a place in Herefordshire.

The Domesday Book lists 49 castles as existing in 1086—and it is Okehampton Castle which is given the distinction of being mentioned in that memorable inventory. An estimated 85 castles existed before the year 1100, only five or six, however, were constructed of stone, since timber was plentiful and easier to work.

That Devon was in a rebellious mood can be gauged from the fact that around twenty castles were erected within the county boundaries by the Normans. Harold's family did pose a threat to the stability which the Conqueror sought. William distributed land in Devon with a lavishness not matched, even, by Henry VIII's gifts to the Bedford family centuries later.

Of the 1,000 or so Domesday estates, some 870 were wrested away from the unfortunates who owned them prior to the Conquest, and given to a half-dozen foreigners.

Exasperating dissent litters the historical period after William's death, but essentially, the carve-up of the spoils of conquest between the handful of Norman families laid the foundation for a new England.

Let us turn to the physical evidence of Norman power—the military deterrent of the eleventh and twelfth centuries—the castle. To the natives of the time they were awesome examples of might—as daunting—though not, of course, with anything like the destructive capacity—as modern-day defences. They kept an uneasy peace—in much the same way, as it is argued, that deterrents of modern times have maintained that desirable state of affairs.

Right: More than a century ago, an observer noted that this ruined fragment of Okehampton Castle appeared to tumble down the slopes. But it is still there.

12

Like all deterrents, however, they eventually became redundant, overtaken by devices capable of inflicting more pain and senseless destruction. By the end of the fourteenth century these seemingly imperishable fortresses—the ultimate deterrents of their time—were being used more for domestic than defence purposes.

The basic function of a Norman castle was three-fold: defence, administration and for private residential purposes. By the time of King Edward III, however, England was largely subdued: Norman and Saxon had been assimilated—the strange and churlish Celts weren't interested. Chambers and chapels, great halls and windows began to appear in castle architecture. Even the barons submitted to the Royal insistence that a licence must be obtained for the crenellation of castle walls.

The castle had become an accepted part of the English scene, and reached its zenith around the year 1322 when there were at least sixty Royal castles in the realm, and every nobleman in England worthy of the name possessed one or more.

The irony of it all was exemplified when King Edward II was incarcerated at Berkeley Castle, on the barons' orders, and savagely done to death there.

There were castles also, we should not forget, in such far-away places as Syria—reminders of our role in the Crusades. Forsaken exiles, as Hugh Braun reminds us, with no green turf or swathes of ivy to temper their loneliness, and with only the whirling dust-devils stalking their courts for garrison.

By Cromwell's time, the occupied English castle was fast becoming a rarity. The Royalists utilised even the ruined shells as focal points for resistance to the ideal of the Commonwealth. Cromwell and his troops showed little enough mercy afterwards to these potential trouble spots—a policy of active destruction followed by one of benign neglect, in much the same manner as the fate which befell the abbeys and monasteries after the Dissolution a century earlier.

To many, the castle was the ready-made stone quarry, as the abbeys had been in their time of downfall. Unlike the many cathedrals which suffered under the contemptible vandalism of the

Left: The splendid tower of Tiverton Castle.

philistine Puritans, however, the castles were never rebuilt or restored. The loss to our heritage was immeasurable as a result.

The mottes (or mounds) survive—even the ignorant louts who stripped the stone for self-gain found no use for these splendid features of Norman building. The baileys became village greens, though some owners wished to plough them into extinction. The moats have, by and large, disappeared. They were created, of course, after the Normans found that their favoured design for square keeps, could be readily undermined by human moles who would burrow beneath the foundations in time of siege, and bring the corners crashing down. Round keeps resulted, with moats of water to keep miners out. I cannot help but think that every successful besieging army would most cheerfully have welcomed a corps of Cornish miners in their midst. Nor, when compiling this book, could I refrain from thinking of the smells which must have emanated from any stagnant circle of water. It is said that seventeenth-century Versailles could be smelled from three miles distant: was it the same with some of our English castles?

But what of our castles today? And, particularly, those of Devon?

The once dread symbols of conquest, of the oppressor and the oppressed, have been transmuted into venerated bulwarks of the English scene, adding lustre to the landscape, and not liability. That is unless you happen to own one, and have to struggle to maintain a crumbling fabric on a shoe-string budget. English Heritage, The National Trust and private individuals are obliged to devise all manner of means to try to preserve these historic monuments, glorious examples of our history and heritage. Designation doesn't provide the wherewithall to conserve their beauty.

Some castles, like other great properties, have become so popular with the public that the human tide of pounding feet threatens their very integrity. Increasingly, it seems, success is measured by the annual number of visitors rather than by the quality of the experience: by income derived, irrespective of the cost of destroying the irreplaceable. Starved of grants, riddled by taxation, it is no wonder that the private owners in particular have been tempted to grasp at modern marketing methods. The regret, however, must lie in the future, with generations as yet unborn.

The castles of Devon are a valuable, loved and wholly delightful portion of our heritage, whether they are a pile of ruins or some still developing entity. They offer a unique educational opportunity, and

14

Building Castle Drogo.

a rich and fulfilling visual experience. As a test of history and imagination, they are unique, and intensely human in their appeal.

In this book I have endeavoured to create a little of the substance from the shadows. Devon has no fantasy in the way of castles to offer. No Caernarvon, no Warwick, nor even a Neuschwanstein, a castle which helped immortalise the hapless Ludwig II of Bavaria—Wagner apart. But there is an excellent variety to be found here—as I hope to demonstrate. Castles where winds have caressed parched stones in the green lap of countless springtimes. Years of sun and rain have scorched and washed them of colour, but to any with imagination their content is of drama and mystery. Fitful masquerades flow through the mind as the sunshine streams upon lordly battlements and illuminates lonely towers.

This book is not intended to be a guide to these feudal monuments, but hopefully, it may lead some to look again, with interest, at what remains.

It is too late to regret that the famous Rougemont, at Exeter,

suffered to make way for an assize hall, but we may be thankful, at least, that the horrific Lydford Castle is no longer a place of imprisonment.

Watermouth Castle has no great history, but there can be few lovelier settings: how the Normans would have adored the rolling woodland for their winter meat supplies.

Barnstaple Castle, with its arthritic beeches crowding its grand motte, must once have presented a rare spectacle, and who can visit it without thinking of Judhael, whose round keep at Totnes magnificently crowns a precipice of fortification.

To wander through the empty halls of Okehampton Castle is an experience not to be missed. Note the holes in its walls, like martins' nests on sandy cliff faces. Cow parsley, like lace curtains, blooms in drifts near the gurgling river. But its ancient deer park is soon to be wreathed with a bypass, by Parliamentary decree.

At Tiverton Castle there lived a Plantagenet Princess, her son only a heart-beat away from becoming King of England. Down in the dell is little Bickleigh Castle where the vagabond spirit of Bampfylde Moore Carew lingers on.

Imperious Drogo, crouching like a Crusader castle on the lip of a Devonshire ravine—is this merely another folly of the twentieth century? Hopefully not.

Pretty Gidleigh—is it pretentious or simply picturesque? The latter, I like to believe.

Then there is Powderham, home of that most remarkable of Devon families, the Courtenays, and sweet Compton, which must stir the heart in every Englishman.

Berry Pomeroy, a truly medieval castle, is quite unforgettable among Devon's castles: odd that so few know where it is.

Plymouth Castle is no more, merely a fragment: the body having been swallowed up in development, and Plympton is a forlorn reminder of Civil War, of Royalists and Roundheads.

Last, but by no means least, in this collection, there are Dartmouth and Kingswear Castles—divided by the opal and sapphire of the wandering waves.

For we, which now behold these present days,
Have eyes to wonder, but lack tongues to praise.

Left: The Norman gateway at Rougemont, Exeter.

Castle Drogo

Spartan granite, hewn and configured into mighty shapes of monumental symmetry, marks Castle Drogo as a place apart. Crouching leopard—crusader castle—call it what you will, it provided a great English architect, Edwin Lutyens, with the opportunity of the age.

Spurred on by the owner, Julius Drewe, Lutyens was entrusted with the awesome task of creating what, in all probability, will become the last castle ever to be built in England.

The site is serene. Drewe laid the foundation stone under the north-east corner of the castle on 4 April 1911. It was nineteen years in the making, and not before Drewe had curbed his architect's taste for creating a full-blown bailey with a crenellated curtain wall and medieval-style gate-house. Lutyens was, doubtless, the only architect who could be entrusted with such a monstrous extravaganza in granite because, suggests Nikolaus Pevsner, he still believed in pomp and circumstance.

But such confusion! The predominant style outside, declares Pevsner, an acknowledged expert in such matters, is Tudor. The vaulting, inside, is Roman, if anything, in character, but the scullery has Norman columns, and there is a vaulted chapel in the basement. Drewe, sharing his architect's exultation in the creation, managed to fill it with a miscellany of objects, ranging from Chinese Chippendale to Hispano-Maroc. And, amazingly, it works!

Even the wonderful gardens at Castle Drogo have an unearthly quality. I well recall an American visitor, her gaze directed upwards towards the pair of trees which stand sentinel-like at the top of the

Right: The chapel at Castle Drogo; reminiscent of the Coptic churches of distant Ethiopia.

A SHOP IN VENICE, *after* BORONONI

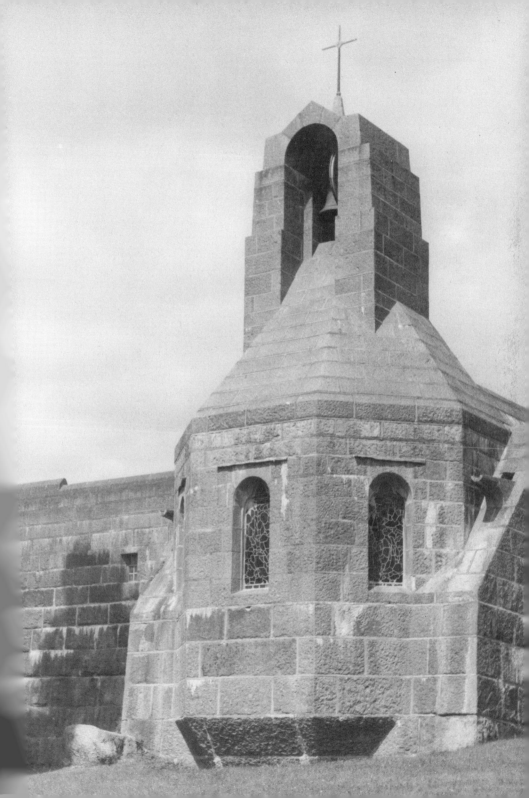

Above: Julius Drewe (centre) and Mrs Drewe (left) with their children and grandchildren. Right: 'Drewe is the name and valour gave it arms.' The grand entrance to Castle Drogo.

stepped garden path, murmuring, as if in a dream: 'Is this the entrance to Valhalla?' The castle had stunned her. What, perhaps, is not immediately evident, is the magnificent symmetry. It is almost as if Castle Drogo had been carved from a single block of stone.

But let us return to its beginnings. Julius Charles Drewe, born into by no means a wealthy family in 1856, was sent to China as a tea buyer. He quickly assessed that by cutting out the middle-man he could buy goods at a reduced price from the country of origin.

He opened his first shop in Liverpool, in 1878, and the business rapidly developed under the name of The Home and Colonial Stores. Soon, he owned a chain of grocer shops, rivalling Sainsbury and Lipton. At the tender age of 33, Drewe was able to retire, leaving others to manage the shops, in which he continued to hold a substantial interest. He was, perhaps, the classic example of what

20

DROGO NOMEN ET VIRTUS ARMA DEDIT

Mrs Margaret Thatcher meant when she referred to Victorian values and enterprise.

Drewe lived the life of a country gentleman at Wadhurst Hall, having acquired with it much of the furniture of the previous owner, Adrian de Murietta, a Spanish banker: hence the Iberian influence upon Castle Drogo's furnishings.

But Drewe had a dream. A genealogist persuaded him that he was descended from a Norman, Drogo or Dru, who had come over with William the Conqueror. He clearly knew of Drewsteignton, the tiny village which nestles around its granite Holy Trinity Church, and in 1910, he purchased the Glebe Lands, which included the site of the present castle, and changed his name by deed poll from Drew to Drewe.

The vision began to take substantial form when Lutyens joined the Drewe family to picnic, and finished up pegging out the site of a potential castle. Lutyens too was enthralled by the enthusiasm of his client. Dream shapes floated through his mind—the imperial majesty of his Delhi creations were yet to come. A gallery 160 feet in length, a chapel rising through three storeys, fireplaces twelve feet wide . . .

It was too much even for Drewe and, years later, some must wonder at Lutyens: he was to know Delhi, but did he understand Dartmoor? 'When a barbarian built a fortress,' wrote Lutyens to the complaining Drewe, 'he heaped up rocks and hid the women behind them.' Drewe pondered, and recorded the fact that he could only be thankful that Lutyens had not seen the Pyramids before he had engaged him on Castle Drogo. The two men, however, continued to be firm friends, and were marvellously matched.

Over the entrance gate a lion—Mr Drewe's—stood sentinel in heraldic style. Beneath it was inscribed the Drewe motto: *Drogo Nomen et Virtus Arma Dedit*—Drewe is the name and valour gave it arms.

Julius Drewe happily lived to see the castle completed, and not until after the War, in 1974, was Castle Drogo given to The National Trust, with 600 acres of surrounding land to ensure the conservation of the magnificent landscape.

In October, 1979, the modern architect, Anthony Hollow reported on the water penetration and dampness in the building making particular reference to the North Tower. As a piece of architecture, he said, Drogo is unique. So too one suspects is the construction of

Symmetry on a summer's day at Castle Drogo.

the building but unfortunately the latter, as opposed to the brilliance of the former, has shortcomings both in design and execution, and the building is not watertight. Water penetration, which the Trust is determined to forestall, was said to be the result of a series of complex causes. On Dartmoor, few people were really surprised: 'Build with a flat roof, and you build for trouble,' reporters were told.

Lutyens had changed his stylistic interpretation from classical romanticism to elementalism, reported the *Architectural Review* of 1979. A compromise.

Was the architect thinking thus when he wrote to his wife, in August 1910: 'Mr Drewe writes a nice and exciting letter. I go on with the drawings.

'Not more than £50,000 tho' and £10,000 for the garden. I suppose £60,000 sounds a lot to you—but I don't know what it means, if I look at Westminster Abbey it is an absurd—a trivial amount . . . only I do wish he did *not* want a castle—but a delicious lovely house with plenty of good large rooms in it.'

But Julius was dreaming more delicious thoughts—a Dartmoor demesne, as Drogo de Teynton, his Norman ancestor would have admired. Edwin reflected on Italy, the great buildings on the hilltops which excited him so fearfully: 'High, high up against the sky—and how the devil do they get to them, still more at them to build them?' he asked himself. But he doodled, with fantasy sketches, to please Drewe, of Drogo de Teynton riding up, on horseback, to enter his great castle.

Out of the shadows came substance. Elementalism it might have been, but Elgar-ish too, with the swagger of pomp and circumstance, not to mention a hint of Wagnerian opulence—a site where the Valkyries would not seem unduly out of place, but above all, we should remember, the last in the line of the castles of Devon and England itself.

Castle Drogo crouches on the skyline; all the glory of a Crusader fortress in a Devon landscape.

Lydford

The former tinners' gaol at Lydford has been contemptuously dismissed as a primitive little keep. The description is accurate, but appearances never were more deceptive.

This unprepossessing cube of stone once played a crucial—and often barbaric—role in the administration of Dartmoor's forest laws and Devon's tin industry. Its very name struck terror in the hearts and minds of innocent and guilty alike: for centuries it was associated with summary justice and dread punishment.

In 1195, a sum of £74 was spent in constructing a strong tower at Lydford to detain those guilty of offending against the forest laws—royal prisoners—for the King or the Earls of Cornwall were Lords of Dartmoor.

This two-storey high 'strong house' was 52-feet square with ten-feet thick walls. Only the ground floor of the original building has survived; the original tower was partly demolished sometime during the thirteenth century, and another two storeys were built on. At the same time, a ditch was dug around the early tower, and earth and stone was heaped around the outside forming the substantial mound which nowadays encircles the castle.

The thinking behind the creation of this motte, or mound, is a mystery. The work could well have been commissioned by Richard, Earl of Cornwall (1227-1272). But why? Certainly it lent an air of might more than dignity to this austere fortress, which now also boasted a bridge across its new ditch between the castle bailey and tower entrance.

The old ground floor was filled in with rubble except, significantly, for a small pit. That was to be a place of chilling horror, an abominable black hole. It could be reached only by ladder—an unlit and dreaded chamber of the damned. The rubble has now been cleared away yet, to this very day, workmen sent down there on ropes to clear away the litter and debris still experience, though only momentarily, the horror of this hell-hole.

For the Dartmoor tinner, Lydford was the hub of the Universe. Their dead souls, decently shriven, were borne along the lonely lych way to Lydford Church, beside which this grim square tower has loomed for eight centuries. The medieval tinner—the immemorial bowed figure of a solitary man working in the vast silence of the moor—as Professor Hoskins has described him—led a rough, short life.

Bread, the brownest; cheese, the hardest; drink, the thinnest; yea, commonly the dew of heaven, which he tasteth either from his shovel, or spade, or in the hollow of his hand . . . wrote a contemporary of this tough breed of men, whose Parliaments, or Courts, met at infrequent intervals on Crockern Tor, Dartmoor (we know of at least thirteen between 1474 and 1786). Lydford was their gaol; justice was summary, punishment was swift, and carried out often well in advance of the deliberations of their infrequent Tinners' Parliamentary meetings. The laws of the forest and those of the tinners were utterly intolerant and invariably intractable in their severity. Lydford law became a national by-word. Lydford castle epitomised its ruthlessness.

In 1510, the Plympton M.P. Richard Strode of Newnham dared to introduce at Westminster a Bill to curb mining operations from clogging up, with their waste, local harbours. The Stannary Court fined him. Strode, a tinner himself, refused to pay. His temerity landed him in Lydford gaol where his experience of incarceration in a deep pit under the ground in the castle of Lydford . . . one of the most heinous, contagious and detestable places within this realm . . . earned him immortality as a founding father of the rights of Parliamentary privilege.

Over a century later, the little Tavistock poet, William Browne, came to Lydford to visit a friend, Colonel James Hals, a Parliamentarian, and prisoner of war. The castle was then in the custody of Sir Richard Grenville, Charles I's general in the west. The sensitive Browne was appalled. His verses on the visit have long survived his other poetry, lovely and inspiring though much of it is.

Keeping company now with gaunt conifers, Lydford prison has a distinctive history of horror.

> *I oft have heard of Lydford law*
> *How in the morn they hang and draw*
> *And sit in judgement after.*
> *At first I wondered at it much,*
> *But since I've found the matter such*
> *That it deserves no laughter.*

Better, he wrote, to be stoned, pressed or hanged than pass a night in that dread pit: 'At six o'clock I came away and pray'd for those that were to stay within a place so arrant: wide and ope the winds so roar, by God's grace I'll come no more 'til forc'd by a tin warrant.'

Shortly after Browne's visit, in 1644, the last execution took place. A man was hanged in chains and left to swing, his body daubed with pitch for preservation, and a Walter Yolland, faithful soldier of the Commonwealth, was starved to death there, 'by the inhumane dealing of the enemy'.

27

'... the notorious Judge Jeffries ...'

Lydford Castle was living up to its reputation!

Its rundown state after the Civil War was, not surprisingly, said to have been wanton and intentional. Prince Charles had spent £100 in 1625 for its necesary repair, but by 1650, a report on the state of

Lydford Borough revealed that the castle was in poor condition. Of the four little rooms, two above stairs, the floors were broken, with main timbers having fallen. The tower roof lead was worth £80 (13,895lbs at three-ha'pence per lb laid over 1,544 square feet) and the timber £6. The stones weren't worth removal.

The tinners, no longer the force they had been, complained that without a gaol their laws were ineffective. Notwithstanding, legend has it that the notorious Judge Jeffries sat in judgement there, despite the fact that his Bloody Assize stopped short of Lydford. His ghost, in the shape of a black pig, is nightly doomed to haunt the scene of his brutality. Such legends die hard.

By 1703, the castle roof was open to the vagaries of weather and, early in the nineteenth century the Vicar of Tavistock, the Reverend Edward Atkyns Bray, noted that, despite the repairs carried out, the stairs and floor of the castle could not be trodden without danger. But the judge's chair remained, complete with royal coat of arms, in perfect preservation.

Bray, as fanciful an author as his Victorian novelist wife, Anna Eliza, reported: 'The infamous Jeffries is reputed to have been the last who presided in it. The only thing that seems to have elevated the judge above the rest of the court is a footboard at the bottom of the chair . . . the counsel table has been removed only within these few years. To the dungeon, which is about sixteen feet by ten, the descent must have been by ladder, and probably through a trap door. If this were the case, it was completely dark, as there is no window in it, and the room above is lightened only by a single narrow loop-hole.'

But its authority had vanished. The royal headquarters had moved on, to Princetown, the new capital of the moor.

Crows now cry from their perches on its jagged walls, ferns luxuriate in the dank interior.

Archaeological investigations during the 1960s and 1970s have revealed more of Lydford's Saxon past and its royal mint.

Antique, ancient Lydford castle, stannary prison, now stands silent, surrounded by neatly cut grass covering both motte and bailey. In 1932, the Duchy of Cornwall placed it in the care of the then Office of Works.

The wind moans around the walls of its keep. It remains now as merely a symbol of oppression; to our forefathers though, it was a castle of terror.

Gidleigh

During the wet month of September, 1918, two keen archaeologists, J.S. Amery and R.H. Worth spent some time exploring Dartmoor. Since the wind was so strong that they were unable to set up their camera tripod on the moor, the two men descended upon Gidleigh, and sheltered within the walls of the castle.

Their report was not published in the *Transactions of the Devonshire Association* until seven years later, but it was almost certainly the first time that anyone had taken a serious interest in this most delightful little castle.

No-one has seemed capable of writing about the castle without employing the words 'pretentious' or 'picturesque'. It is, of course, both, but in a particularly English manner—almost as if created by a real eccentric.

It was constructed, it would seem—though no-one can be certain—at about the time the Courtenays began to create their mighty fortress at Okehampton. The general consensus among historians and archaeologists is that Gidleigh Castle was contemporary with the Courtenay building at Okehampton— though not on such a grand scale. According to Risdon, it was created by Sir William Prouse, who died during 1315 or 1316. Not that this helps much, except in so far as demonstrating that even in those far-off days of the big, bad barons, there were some men who plainly believed that small could be beautiful.

Gidleigh Castle is a fortress in miniature—a pocket edition of a castle.

Even Amery and Worth were moved to write in their scholarly treatise: 'We admit a certain sentimental sympathy with the knight, who finding his family estates enhanced by the judicious matrimonial ventures of his ancestors (the Courtenays) launched out in emulation of his greater neighbours, and, having built such

The tiny but picturesque castle at Gidleigh, on Dartmoor.

lordly residence as the depth of his purse would permit, went his way, leaving no male heir to continue the name.'

But the family of Prouse did not, fortunately, die with him. He had a daughter, Lady Alice de Moelis and to an old father nothing is more sweet.

There are many details common to the architecture of both Okehampton and Gidleigh castles—jamb chamfers, stone from the same quarry which, after six centuries of wear and tear and weather, still bears the impression of tool marks and is, if anything, even warmer and lovelier in the tone of old age than the day it was quarried from Hatherleigh.

The keep, if it will bear such an imposing description, consists only of a cellar, with three splendid ribbed arches, and a solar, or private room at first-floor level. Once, it boasted a lead roof and parapet, but no longer. The stairway is well worn from the passage of time's footsteps, and diminutive—merely six feet in diameter. Once, it must have led to the roof. Unfortunately, late last century,

31

when the ground nearby was levelled for the garden of the Castle House, the effect was to undermine the walls.

Amery and Worth reported that the turret stairway was ruined, cracked from top to bottom, and inefficiently propped with a pole: the entrance arch had fallen, and the stair newel collapsed. The east wall was ruined. Their paper to the Devonshire Association clearly stimulated some essential repair work and today the castle stands four square and firm—although tufts of valerian have gained a foothold, and through the moss the ivies creep . . .

Sir William, who built it, also copied the Courtenays of Okehampton by creating a deer park, or chase. Was he a short, rotund squire (that narrow stairwell) who revelled in country pursuits? And was his castle a little larger than what we may see above ground level today?

In Victorian times, its then owner, the Reverend Dr Whipham, who purchased it in 1819 under a decree of Chancery—the last of the Gidley family having sold it in the latter part of the eighteenth century—said he had found a quantity of freestone in old buildings in the locality, which seems to have originated from mullion windows from the castle. According to tradition, a subterranean passage leads from the castle to the River Teign. Such stories are not uncommon where castles are concerned.

The Reverend Sabine Baring-Gould called it a doll's castle! But it was built at a time when such men as John Wycliffe were advising lords to lead a rightful life, keeping the hests of God, doing the works of mercy, ruling well the five wits, and doing reason and equity and good conscience to all men. Labourers were exhorted to live in meekness!

We know, however, that Gidleigh Castle and the nearby church, lay directly upon the so-called Mariners' Way across Dartmoor—the path taken by sailors changing ship between the ports of South Devon, Dartmouth say, and the North, Bideford for example. The charitable people of this lovely old Devon village of Gidleigh gave money to the matelots as they wound a way through. The Church-wardens' accounts show expenditure of one shilling in 1760 ('Gave a sailor that had a pass') and sixpence in 1774 ('Giv'd alms to sailor'). Jolly Jack Tar was welcome at Gidleigh.

The castle is also supposed to harbour a ghost or two, including one of a white horse. That may have some substance in fact, since a farmer was supposed to have hidden the animal in the cellar to escape the attention of bailiffs. The horse, which ought not to have been there, was in the habit, so it is said, of taking the air through the cellar door at dusk—the origin of such 'ghost' stories is plain.

There is, today, a wonderful sense of timelessness about this castle, and its lovely gardens, whose stone walls may owe much to the materials so readily available from the source nearby.

It is owned by Mr and Mrs Michael Hardy, who have lived at Castle House for three years, and adore it, and the castle. It is, then, situated on private property, and anyone wishing to explore the castle should write, in advance, seeking the permission of the owners.

Built at around the same time as Okehampton Castle, and with its own deer park nearby, Gidleigh Castle was never as pretentious a place as its neighbour.

Okehampton

The halls of Okehampton's once great castle are now naked ruins. Fitful blasts of wind gust down upon this splendid craggy knoll from Dartmoor's vast wilderness, stirring the handsome trees, and threatening still to topple, once and for all, the towering remnants of the Norman keep perched precariously on the conical motte.

As long ago as 1848 Samuel Rowe, perambulating Dartmoor, wrote that 'one lofty fragment appears ready to tumble down headlong at the first assault of the blustering tempests from the neighbouring wilds of Dartmoor; but from the durable qualities of the cement, it has withstood the fury of the elements and may, we trust, long stand to add interest and beauty to this charming scene.' To see it to perfection, added Rowe, the tourist should visit it by pale moonlight. Interesting advice—for surely Rowe knew of the celebrated ghostly presence said to haunt Okehampton.

My lady's coach hath nodding plumes
The driver hath no head;
My lady is an ashen white
Like one that is long dead.

My Lady was, of course, Lady Howard of Fitzford, Tavistock, a woman of great character who is said to haunt this place as a penance for her misdeeds. What were these? She was an 'unnatural mother' whispered the Victorian gossips. Modern-day investigation, however, reveals that Mary Howard's own mistreatment at the hands of her sadistic father, Sir John Fitz, could well have robbed her of the normal maternal instincts.

Right: Lady Howard of Fitzford: 'Legend has it that at the hour of midnight she sets forth in a coach of bones . . .'

The ruined chapel and priest's lodgings.

Legend has it that at the hour of midnight, she sets forth in a coach of bones from Fitzford Gatehouse, Tavistock, with the four grinning skulls of her husbands decorating each corner. Before her runs a coal-black hound, all the way to Okehampton Castle, where the hound must pluck a blade of grass which it carries back and lays upon a stone which once stood in the courtyard of Fitzford House. When all the grass of Okehampton Castle shall have been brought back to Tavistock, the penance of the wicked Lady Howard shall cease.

There are several versions of this tale—but it is as firmly-established a legend as any in Devon.

> *Now pray slip in, my Lady saith*
> *Now pray slip in, and ride . . .*
> *There's room, I trow, by me, for you*
> *And all the world beside.*

Beneath the moon's light, there is an eerie quality to Okehampton Castle.

But let us return to fact from fancy. Okehampton seems to have been one of the few created by the Normans on an entirely new site. 'There stands a castle' the Domesday scribe recorded in 1086 of a building created some eighteen years earlier on the instructions of Baldwin de Brionne, Sheriff of Devon.

Baldwin made Okehampton the headquarters of his huge tally of Devon manors, scattered far across the county—a reward from William the Conqueror, with whom he had plotted the conquest of England, and whose cousin, Emma, he had married. Baldwin was known by many titles—Baldwin de Meules (or Meulles) or de Sap and later as Baldwin of Exeter, as we shall see from the chapter on Rougemont. On his death, in about 1090, his estates passed to his three sons, William, Robert and Richard who, like their father, had wide-ranging interests in England and France.

But Okehampton Castle was the symbol, and the instrument, of feudal power. Even today, in its ruinous state, it is not difficult to imagine how it would have struck wonder and awe into the hearts of the common people. Baldwin had it built on a great spur of shale in the valley of the West Okement river. By 1173, his last surviving heiress, Hawisia, married Reginald Courtenay, which began that noble family's 365-year-long occupancy of the castle which ended in tragedy, as we shall see.

Although, in 1274, the castle was described as 'an old motte which is worth nothing, and outside the motte a hall, chamber and kitchen poorly built' Okehampton Castle entered upon its golden age in the following century. The Courtenays poured power and affection upon it, utilising the space to the south as a great deer park, and from 1335, the family, of whom it has been written: 'No pedigree in England, and very few in Europe, can vie with that of the Earls of Devon, and unlike most it is not of herald's manufacture' reigned supreme. There was no lay landowner to rival them, and possession of Tiverton, Plympton and Okehampton Castles added to their might. We shall meet them again, at Powderham, this century.

But they crashed, mightily, in 1538, when Henry Courtenay, then Marquess of Exeter, incurred the deadly, violent wrath of his cousin, and boyhood companion, Henry VIII, and stood accused of conspiracy with Cardinal Pole and the papists. Courtenay, along with Neville, Carew and Montague, was executed. His son, Edward

Courtenay, seemingly the last Earl, until fate intervened centuries later, flirted with the Princess Elizabeth and by so doing, incurred the jealousy of her sister Queen Mary, who had evidently considered him a fit match for her own hand. After imprisonment in the dread Fotheringay Castle, and Mary's marriage to Philip of Spain, Edward was released, only to be exiled to Padua, far from Okehampton Castle, and where, on foreign soil, he died in mysterious circumstances—poisoned, it is said—in 1556. One of Europe's most illustrious families appeared to have been extinguished.

Henry Courtenay's alleged treason meant the estates reverted to the crown and, from that moment, it seemed, the great castle of Okehampton began its long decline towards ruin.

The castle, decaying slowly, was used for more mundane purposes down the corridor of centuries, as R.A. Higham's excellent guide reveals. At the beginning of the twentieth century it was owned by a local benefactor, Sydney Simmons, who carried out restoration work and granted it, in 1917, to the Okehampton Castle Trust. In 1967 it came into the guardianship of the Ministry of Public Buildings and Works, and is now cared for by English Heritage, who have put much thought and skill into its continued preservation.

If ruins can be described as splendid, which seems a contradiction in itself, then Okehampton Castle falls into that category. Memories of past glories flash across the mind, like the glance of sunlight upon ancient rocks: Baldwin, the Courtenays, and even Celia Fiennes who, unromantically, rode into Okehampton in 1698—some 21 years after Lady Howard's death—drenched to the skin 'the wettest day I had in all my summer's travels hitherto!'

Modern man is now busily devising an Okehampton bypass to carry the noisome toil of traffic away from the beleaguered main street upon a new road to be pitched high above the crumbling square keep of the castle and through its ancient deer park. The battle by the conservationists has rumbled around these ruins, but the road lobby seems to have won the day.

But here is a riddle for the reader. She was courted by Devon and Somerset, who paid dearly for their interest, but she rejoiced, always, in her brother Cornwall's company. Who was she? Okehampton Castle provides part of the answer.

Powderham

The Courtenays, whom we met at Okehampton, have a long and noble lineage, and can trace their name back to the year 1000 and to a castle which they built south of Paris.

This French branch intermarried with the royal house of Valois, and produced three Emperors of Constantinople during the times of the Fourth Crusade. The English line began with Reginald de Courtenay who came over, not, like so many French noblemen, with the Conqueror, but with the remarkable Eleanor of Aquitaine, bride of King Henry II. He married Hawisia, last of the de Brionnes, as we saw, and became Baron of Okehampton and Sheriff of Devon. In 1335 his family inherited the Earldom of Devon from their grand cousins, the de Redvers.

At Powderham, on the banks of the Exe, the Domesday lord was William of Eu, a rebel, whom the strange and terrible William Rufus blinded and castrated in 1096. Some 300 years later, the estate was presented to Sir Philip Courtenay by his father, the second Earl of Devon, and his mother, Margaret de Bohun. This branch of the family flourished even when the last Earl perished from poison in 1556. It was Sir Philip who began the construction of Powderham Castle around 1390 and, although battered about somewhat during the Civil War, and deserted by the receding River Exe, it has been the Courtenay home for an astonishing continuous period of almost 600 years. Even rarer, indeed, is the unbroken male descent for such a time; yet from 1556 until 1831 the Courtenays, it seemed, were oblivious to their right of title to the Earldom of Devon.

Artists and architects, poets and priests, musicians and builders—but above all the owners—created a sumptuous home at Powderham, where the patronage was on a scale befitting a noble family. Visit the castle and see for yourself.

*Above: The Earl and Countess of Devon with their son,
Lord Courtenay (centre). Right: '. . . Powderham lives on
complete . . .'*

The medieval core has been embellished down the six centuries as
the individual Baronets and Viscounts stamped their mark upon
their home. The purists are sometimes appalled, but purists usually
are. Nikolaus Pevsner, for example, is dismissive of the 'operatic'
forecourt composition by Fowler: even *Murrays Guide* in 1859
complained that the walls looked too fresh in their new coats of
plaster. What they ignore is the fact that this is a house and a home,
and if, as is the case, a TV aerial is seen projecting from a castellated
roof-top, we should, perhaps, before condemning such sights as
incongruous, give thanks that Powderham lives on complete, and
not in ruins like many of its great contemporary castles.

The story of how the Earldom of Devon was restored to its
rightful owners is worth the retelling.

When Edward Courtenay was restored to his ancestors' honours
in 1553 by Queen Mary, what was virtually a new Earldom was

created. A careless clerk omitted three words, *de suo corpore* (of his body) from the letters patent, which opened the way for even the most distant of relatives to inherit the title. Not until 1830 was the error noted by an assistant clerk of the Parliaments at Westminster, who happened to be a cousin of the Courtenays, and heir to the third Viscount, William. The House of Lords decided the claim to the title was justified, and the Earldom of Devon was restored, in 1831, albeit as the fifth in British seniority, and not the first.

For all the wonders of Powderham Castle—the superb staircase—over which the experts still drool in admiration—and the grand imposing halls, the music room, designed by James Wyatt for the third Viscount (and first of the restored Earls) stands out. Within it hangs the Richard Cosway portrait of the third Viscount in masquerade costume for his coming-of-age party in 1791—a most lavish affair which portended the shape of things to come.

The second Viscount and his wife had thirteen daughters and one son, William. One of the daughters, Elizabeth, eloped in 1788, but if this Jane Austen-style situation was not bad enough, then William, the third Viscount, became involved in a reputed homosexual liaison, involving the notorious William Beckford, which scandalised the neighbourhood and cast a cloud over the Courtenays of that time. Hugely talented as he was, but a spendthrift also, William, hounded by gossips and debts left England first for New York then Paris, when he died, unmarried, but not unmourned or indeed forgotten, in 1835.

Lady Paulina Pepys, in an *English Life* publication, has written, of the music room, that where the organ stands there was, at one time, a stage stretching back into the room behind, and many plays and operettas were performed there: 'On one occasion, the third Viscount is said to have popped up through a hole in the floor dressed as the devil and nobody, so the story goes, was in the least bit surprised.'

Powderham is best described as a fortified manor house rather than a fully-fledged castle—and there appears to be no evidence, despite the claims of some authors, that any castle existed here before Sir Philip Courtenay (who died in 1406) began the building around 1390. Until the latter part of the eighteenth century, the River Exe ran near the east wall of Powerham, and its tributary the River Kenn, almost touched the southern walls.

It was Hilaire Belloc who described the English castle as one of the most illuminating objects of study in history. They fell, he suggested, into three categories—a ruin, a restoration, or a fragment onto which has been grafted a later dwelling house unsuited to war. Powderham falls into that latter category, stoutly even unexpectedly though it did resist the advance of Fairfax in the Civil War.

Old Froissart, marching with an army in the days when Powderham was hardly a twinkle in the bright eyes of the Courtenays, has mentioned, with relish, his obvious enjoyment when the watchmen spied a castle ahead. 'He sounded his horn so agreeably that it was quite a pleasure to hear him.'

We may still enjoy the faint echoes from those cheerful fanfares down six centuries at Powderham. 'The splendour falls on castle walls,' wrote Tennyson, 'and snowy summits old in story: the long light shakes across the lakes, and the wild cataract leaps in glory. Blow, bugle, blow, set the wild echoes flying, blow bugle; answer, echoes, dying, dying, dying.'

*More a fortified manor house than a fully-fledged castle,
Powderham has, nonetheless, been home to the Courtenay family
for nigh on 600 years.*

Totnes

The Normans, or so it might appear, built their castles with the same sort of burning conviction that inspired the Romans to build their roads—to last a thousand years. But we would have difficulty in recognising, as a castle, the simple wood and earth structures which the Conqueror's companions threw up in the eleventh century. These were mere embryos of the proud fortresses in stone which were to follow.

Totnes Castle is a perfect example of how the Normans impressed themselves upon the local populace. It was Judhael, or Juhellus, son of Alured, a Breton, who came over with William after the battle of Hastings to help subjugate the South West. And it was to him that we owe the creation of the early Totnes Castle: doubtless, Judhael was well appraised of the town's importance as one of Devon's quartet of Anglo-Saxon Boroughs—Lydford, Barnstaple and Exeter being the others—and that Totnes, like Lydford, had once boasted its own Mint.

Judhael was plainly a pious man and, as we shall see from his association with Barnstaple, he was to create not only castles, but also priories in both towns. But he backed the wrong man in the struggle between Robert, the eldest son of the Conqueror, and William Rufus—to whom the English throne had been bequeathed. Judhael was driven into exile in 1088, and although he came back into favour under Henry I, and was granted the honour of Barnstaple, Totnes was granted to the de Nonants.

Judhael died in 1123, or thereabouts, at an advanced age. A descendant of his, William de Broase, recovered the family fortunes

Left: Through the gate at Totnes Castle; a walk which takes us from twentieth to twelfth century in a few strides.

almost a century later. But in quicksilver succession, the castle changed hands until, in 1219, Reginald de Broase regained control and, it seems, began to rebuild the castle in stone.

But Reginald himself died childless and left Totnes to his sister, Eva, wife of William de Cantilupe, one of the great lords of the Welsh marches. Then William's son, George, died childless in 1273, and Totnes passed into the hands of another great landowning family, the de la Zouches. It was William de la Zouche who restored the empty and ruinous old castle around 1326, having first assisted in the imprisoning of the pitiful King Edward II—who was to meet his death at Berkeley Castle a year later in grotesque circumstances. The de la Zouches did not live at Totnes, but they held on to the castle until 1485 when the battle of Bosworth settled many an English score: 'I have,' said Richard III, according to Shakespeare, 'set my life upon a cast, and I will stand the hazard of a die . . .'

Totnes Castle was given to Richard Edgcumbe, the young and personable master of Cotehele House, Cornwall, whose daring escape from the Yorkist faction by means of a legendary cliffside leap is celebrated among stories of the River Tamar. About 1559, Totnes Castle was sold off to the Seymours of Berry Pomeroy, who owned it until 1947. It was then that the Duke of Somerset placed it in the guardianship of the Ministry of Works—now English Heritage.

The motte, or mound, is a magnificent structure, and one of the largest in the country. To stand beneath it, or in the tree-clad greenery on its eastern flank, is to experience a remarkable sense of the vastness and echo from the past—a heavy aroma of things ancient hangs over it. The motte's base is hewn from rock, but the great bulk of this mound consists of artificial pounded earth covered with a layer of puddled clay. To those ancient Englishmen who laboured upon its creation, it must have seemed as momentous a task as constructing a pyramid. The lovely shell keep, which radiates like a rosary around its top, has six-feet-thick walls, and is 70 feet in diameter. The keep has 33 merlons, or crenellations, in its wall.

Totnes, as a town, is one of the treasures of England, and its castle is, surely, its crowning glory. The irony, of course, lies in the fact that it was originally created to terrorise the townsfolk. The castle is a classic, and an exquisite example of the motte and bailey

Strolling around the ramparts at Totnes Castle.

design, although historians have searched in vain for records linking the town's story with that of the castle. The owners appeared, in the main, to have been absentee landlords, with the exception of its founder, Judhael. We know, for example, that the sweet fruit of the River Dart graced his table. The annual salmon dues ranged from 80 fish at Dartington to 30 at Loddiswell. Doubtless, the nobleman was to enjoy similar pleasures from the Taw and the Torridge when he moved north to Barnstaple.

From the rampart walk within the shell keep there are splendid views over the Devon countryside: true, the town creeps closer to the walls, with a variety of modern-day Englishman's castles elbowing each other for space, not always altogether as visually attractive as those in the town centre. Like almost every other English Burgh, Totnes was 'saddled' with a Norman castle. The wheel has almost come full circle—now, it seems, it is the castle itself which is threatening to become saddled!

Barnstaple

Mature trees ring the lonely motte of Barnstaple Castle like a wreath. On an autumn morning, when vaporous mists steal in from the nearby River Taw, shrouding the skirt of yellow-brown leaves in a clammy cloak, the mound looms mysterious and foreboding—but at such moments, we may imagine, if only briefly, how this castle might have appeared in its prime, many centuries ago.

It was old Judhael of Totnes, having weathered the clash of the Conqueror's sons, who moved north into this remote outpost of Devon and established a castle here upon a mound some 60 feet tall and 40 feet broad at its crest. Judhael, perhaps, was responsible for substituting stone in place of the timber pile surmounting the earthworks—in which case, Barnstaple may well have resembled Totnes: a lovely circular shell keep with crenellations like a rope of pearls strung around its neck.

We know that when Judhael was visited by a party of monks from the Cluniac monastery of Laon in 1113—a red letter day for this forceful but deeply pious old man—he was actually living in the castle. He had previously founded a priory outside the castle walls. Proudly, he must have pointed out his achievements to his fellow-countrymen from over the Channel and, maybe, after a Te Deum had been sung, made reference to the Bishop of Countances (Geoffrey de Mowbray) who had died twenty years previously, and who may well have established the first castle at Barnstaple.

Was it de Mowbray who laid waste 23 houses on this Taw-side site to create room for a castle? No-one can be certain.

But let us travel forward in time eight centuries, to 1927, when the castle of Barnstaple was purchased by the Corporation, and provided archaeologist Bruce Oliver with an opportunity to dig up the past. They found the moat, some fourteen feet deep, and the site of a cemetery, thereby correcting an earlier impression that human

The tree clad motte at Barnstaple, once crowned by a circular stone keep of Norman times.

skeletons found in 1882 were those of eighteen prisoners hanged upon the castle green in 1590. On top of the motte, or mound, the archaeologists made the major discovery of the foundations of a keep, roughly circular, and consisting of two concentric walls 'very similar to the Keep at Totnes'. The stones were small—some appear to have originated from the Westward Ho! pebble ridge, with sea shells still adhering to them. It was a typical motte and bailey castle of the Norman style.

Bruce Oliver concluded that it was not the wily old Judhael who built the great keep atop the mound at Barnstaple, but a later owner, Henry de Tracey, 'a skilled soldier oft approved in hazards of war' who was a staunch supporter of King Stephen, during whose reign there were several castles built in North Devon—at Loxhore, Parracombe, Torrington and Wembworthy. What's more, argues Mr Oliver, besides the motte and inner bailey, Barnstaple Castle also boasted an outer bailey, to the south of the mound.

We are told that the only known contemporary description of the castle is contained in an Inquisition post-mortem on the death of the last Henry de Tracey in 1274. The words ring down the ages, bridging the centuries: 'There is a certain place which is called the castle about which the wall is almost fallen, and there is a Motte in which there is a certain hall, chamber, kitchen, and other houses closely built, and the easements of the Court without are worth sixpence.'

Half a century earlier, in 1228, the Sheriff of Devon had ordered the walls of Barnstaple Castle to be reduced to a height of ten feet. The King was bothered about the powers of such noblemen. After the last de Tracey's death, the people of Barnstaple made hay with the castle walls. Timber and stone were carted away, and one Michael the Helyer (thatcher) made off with the lead. He died in prison.

By May, 1326, at the post-mortem on William Martyn, the castle was in a ruinous state. Three centuries later, in 1601, part of the remaining wall blew down. The castle had come to a sorry pass considering that the walls were once ten feet thick and eight feet tall. The decay had set in from the time of the last de Tracey: it was, of course, a de Tracey—perhaps a distant relative of this nobleman of North Devon—who was involved in the murder of Thomas à Becket at Canterbury.

As the centuries have slipped away, the nakedness of the mound has become more obvious. Lois Lamplugh, in her outstanding history of Barnstaple (Phillimore, 1983) explains how in June 1727 there was a bonfire on the castle mound and the lessee, named Hiern, objected to this trespass and brought an action against the Borough.

The mount, or hill 'where anciently a castle stood, but no remains thereof are left' provides a clue to its state in the eighteenth century. The people of Barnstaple were, no doubt, celebrating the accession of King George II that June—or, perhaps, the death of his unpopular father, who died on the Continent after eating melons which brought on indigestion.

The bailey—or castle green—has always been a favourite haunt and leisure area for generations of North Devon folk. Nowadays, that too is hemmed in by road traffic and development. The old mound remains, as sturdy a spectacle as it ever was although, sadly, the short but interesting circular walk around its base has been marred by senseless graffiti on the walls and neglect of the footpath itself.

Barnstaple Castle shares with John Dyer's Grongar Hill, the transient smile of Fate: 'A little rule, a little sway, a sun-beam on a winter's day, is all the proud and mighty have between the cradle and the grave.'

Exeter

Exeter Castle, or Rougemont as it is better known, owes its very existence to William the Conqueror. 'The Norman aristocracy, Scandinavian by origin, retained all the Viking energy in colonisation and in war, but had become converts to Latin culture.' In that sentence, the great historian, G.M. Trevelyan brilliantly summed up the Norman spirit, which was to see its feudal flowering not only through heavy armed cavalry, but in the private castles and, not least, the great cathedrals of England.

In the critical years following the conquest—and William's claims to the English throne were at least equal to those of Harold, despite his bastardy—Exeter, influenced by Harold's mother, Githa, refused to admit the Normans. After all, this was the proud city where Caesar himself had once held sway and where, now, the royal House of Godwin was in command. Exeter was the tenth largest city in England, and its 2,500 inhabitants had no intention of meekly surrendering to this Norman upstart.

William, having permitted himself the luxury of returning to Normandy in 1067, to receive the plaudits of his people, left his new kingdom in the care of his turbulent and brutal brother, Odo, Bishop of Bayeux. But he was obliged to hurry back to deal first with insurrection in Kent, and then in 1068, in the far Westcountry.

The king, leading a glittering array of armed cavalry, appeared before the city's Gate. He tried a ploy which was a favourite of all besieging armies—the presentation of a blinded hostage, the dire warning of what would follow if the siege was not lifted immediately. Exeter's response, so Devon historian Professor W.G.

Right: Rougemont, Exeter, the remains of a royal stronghold and a stout reminder of the Norman conquest and architecture.

Hoskins tells us, was an obscene gesture from an uncouth defender. The siege, however, was short-lived.

Eighteen days later it suited William and his followers to agree to an honourable surrender. The city capitulated on the basis that its citizens were not to be harmed or its tribute increased. William, it is said, swore to keep his part of the bargain on the sacred books of the old Exeter Cathedral, then situated near the present building's Lady Chapel. But before he hurried away to deal with the Cornish, William and his engineers decided upon a site for the present castle and, the remaining gatehouse which there arose at Rougemont, or red hill, has been subsequently described as one of the finest pieces of Norman military architecture in England.

Githa, it is said, fled, with her treasure, to Flanders. But Exeter flourished and, a century later, it had become the fourth largest city in the realm after London, York and Winchester. By 1112, the new cathedral, in freshly-cut Beer stone, was begun, and the 48 houses which William the Conqueror's military experts had demolished on the volcanic hill to make room for Exeter Castle were not missed at all.

William left Exeter in the care of Baldwin de Brionne, son of Earl Gilbert, whom he created Sheriff of Devon. The construction of this principal Norman stronghold took many years, but by 1136, it was sufficiently advanced to withstand another great siege in the dispute for the throne between Matilda, daughter of King Henry I, and Stephen, the king's nephew. The then Earl of Devon, Baldwin de Redvers—a family which figures prominently in the construction of the county's castles—supported Matilda, and held out against Stephen's forces for three months.

One of the most effective means of gaining entry to seemingly impregnable castles was to mine their foundations. And this is what Stephen's men tried to do at Exeter, having stormed the castle's outworks. The besiegers worked down from a shaft-head in the trenches until they got below the foundations of the castle wall. They then began to remove foundation stones, replacing them with props of timber, until they had excavated a large chamber. This would then be stuffed up with brushwood, timber and other combustible material which, when fired, would bring down the

Left: Royal Rougemont peeps coyly above the trees at Exeter.

props and the underground roof and with it, hopefully, the castle wall. Two classic examples of success in this undermining were at Rochester, in 1215 and Bedford in 1224. The technique was to lead to the construction of round rather than rectangular keeps in castle building, and the creation of defensive moats of water.

Stephen's army failed to mine the Rougement in 1136. But eight centuries later, when the old Hippodrome building was demolished, in the 1930s, and the ground was being prepared for the foundation of a new building, a tunnel was discovered running from outside the city wall towards the castle. It was almost certainly created by the mining moles of King Stephen's time.

What finally beat the besieged was water shortage: their wells ran dry—another twentieth century phenomenon! Baldwin was lightly let off, in a manner which his grandfather, under William the Conqueror, could never have expected. His estates were confiscated and he was exiled, but within five years he had made peace with the King, came back to live at Corfe Castle, and, what is more, resumed his honour as Earl of Devon. In 1141 he founded the little priory of St James, just outside Exeter.

Exeter Castle continued to feature in national history: Edward III, for instance, incorporated it in his creation of the Duchy of Cornwall for his son, The Black Prince. But one of the strangest of its stories involved the visit to the city by Richard III, shortly after his coronation at York, in 1483. Richard, uncertain of what sort of reception he would be given by Westcountrymen, came to Exeter where, having been cordially received by the Mayor, was shown the castle.

What happened then is recorded for all time by Shakespeare. For Richard, having been told that the name of the castle was Rougemont, re-acted in an extraordinary manner. 'He fell suddenly into a great dump, as it were a man amazed' and Shakespeare recorded the scene thus in his play, *Richard III*:

> *'Richmond! When I was last in Exeter*
> *The Mayor in courtesy showed me the castle*
> *And called it Rougemont—at which name I started,*
> *Because a Bard of Ireland told me once*
> *That I should not live long after I saw Richmond.'*

Rougemont and Richmond were, it appears, looked upon as forms of the same name. And it was, of course, Henry Tudor, Earl of Richmond, marching under the red-dragon standard of Cadwallader, who fulfilled that prophecy at Bosworth Field on 22 August 1485.

Exeter sustained other sieges, of Perkin Warbeck in 1497, and of rebels in 1549. One of its worst features was its gaol, which could compete with that at Lydford for intimidation. It was described as a living tomb—a sink of filth, pestilence and profligacy. Prisoners died there of starvation and in 1585, during the Lent Assizes, Judge Flowerby, eleven jurymen and five magistrates perished of fever contacted, it is alleged, from the pestilential prison.

By the reign of King Charles I, proud Rougemont was described as an 'old ruyning castle whose gaping chinks and aged countenance presageth a downfall ere long.' That downfall came late in the eighteenth century, when the Devon Assize Hall and Sessions House was built over the site.

And so the castle which received one king at its south gate (William the Conqueror) and another at its west (William of Orange) had all but disappeared. Malodorious and ancient, nasty and noisome, though it may have been, the 'vandals' of the eighteenth century, no less destructive and undiscerning than those of our own times, put paid to all except outer walls and gatehouse. That is a rare and precious survival, worth a hundred pompous court houses and a thousand ugly, oily car parking spaces.

Berry Pomeroy

Memories of two great families—the Pomeroys and the Seymours—dance like wisps among the melancholy, but scenic ruins, of Berry Pomeroy Castle. The bulky Pomeroy pile has been penetrated by the once exquisitely romantic creation of the Seymours—bludgeon and flashing rapier architecturally intermingled, a wholly unforgettable spectacle to the modern eye. Two castles intertwined.

On the foggy morning of 5 November, 1689, the fleet of William of Orange bearing the Protestant deliverer approached Torbay. It is said the Prince paused, saying: 'If I am welcome, come and carry me ashore,' whereupon a little man plunged into the waves and carried his future monarch to dry land upon his shoulders. Up the hill rode William with Mareschal Schomberg and divers knights, lords and gentlemen: colours flying, trumpets sounding, hautboys playing, drums beating . . . the Catholics, thinking it the French Fleet landing, sang a Te Deum.

At Berry Pomeroy, Sir Edward Seymour, industrious leader of the so-called 'country party' consulted a hastily-convened meeting of county magnates. There was little support for King James II. William was welcome. But Edward Seymour, as fate would have it, was to be the last resident of Berry Pomeroy castle and, as so many who believe in Divine retribution would have it, the Almighty struck the palatial mansion with lightning and destroyed it to mark His disapproval that the divinity of the Stuart monarchs had been thus terminated.

The Pomeroys came over with the Conqueror. Ralph was granted

Right: A fragment from the glory that was Seymour's Berry Pomeroy.

107 manors in Devon, but of much greater note was the fact that the family was to own Berry for half-a-millennium until finally selling the site, in 1548, for £4,000 to the Seymours, Dukes of Somerset.

About 1300, the splendid gatehouse with its two flanking towers was constructed near the site of a medieval manor house. Unlike many of their Norman contemporaries in Devon, the Breton family of Pomeroys had selected a fairly remote but superbly sheltered site for their home on the lip of a ravine. Many times during their 500 years at Berry the family fell foul of their monarch, narrowly escaping extinction.

Henry de la Pomeroy, for example, supported John Lackland against Richard Coeur de Lion and, having been forced to flee Berry, seized the nigh-impregnable St Michael's Mount in Cornwall, and grimly held out there until all hope was gone. Henry, having assigned his land to his sons, then ordered his surgeon to bleed him to death, in the fashion of the patrician Romans. More colourful legend, however, insists that Henry, in splendid armour, chose to blindfold his horse, and, blowing his bugle in defiance, charged over the precipice at Berry Pomeroy to be dashed to death on the rocks far below.

Little wonder the castle has its ghosts! Another tale would have us believe that long ago, when the sunny corners beneath the castle walls were gay with flowers, a son of the Pomeroys surprised his sister with an enemy of the family. How or when he slew them is not known. But on moonlit nights, the silver glimmer falling through a high embrasure reveals two figures, a man and a woman, pitifully struggling to reach and touch each other across the empty space, yet held back by some power stronger than their love.

Not so long ago, ivy had gained a foothold throughout this twin ruin—through its grassy courts and old chimneys, its broken arches, dungeons, underground passages and crumbling steps. In recent years, archaeologists uncovered a miraculously preserved wall painting, dating, probably from the fifteenth century, when this was Pomeroy property, of the Adoration of the Magi. Subtly, a roof has been created over this corner of the gate house to conserve this treasure which, for three centuries, lay hidden beaneath a great bank of green moss!

Right: The gatehouse at Berry Pomeroy.

The religious convulsions in the first half of the sixteenth century obliged the Pomeroys to sell their stout fortress in the west to Lord Protector Somerset, the pivot of so many cabals and intrigues that it has been argued, wrongly, that the Pomeroys sold Berry Pomeroy to him to save their necks. Somerset's will was quite extraordinary, for he had, when devising his own patent for the dukedom, included the astounding clause that his title should pass to his younger son and not to Edward, his first-born. Only, he willed, when the male issue of the younger son should die out, would the elder's have a reversionary right of succession.

But he left Berry Pomeroy to Edward, his elder son. And, when, several generations later, William of Orange after landing at Torbay commented: 'I think, Sir Edward, that you are of the family of the Duke of Somerset,' Seymour was quick to reply, 'Pardon me, your Highness, the Duke of Somerset is one of *my* family.' A pretty paradox. Time set matters to right and, in 1750, on the death of the Duke of Somerset, without sons to succeed, the honour descended upon the line of the eldest son, and has remained so to this day.

However, the Seymours, having spent at least £20,000 in creating a palatial mansion within the curtain walls of the ancient Pomeroy residence, and living there for part of the seventeenth century, moved their seat to Wiltshire, clearly more accessible to London for Sir Edward Seymour (1633-1708) who was Speaker in the House of Commons.

The deserted house, silent and foreboding, was struck by lightning, and rapidly fell into decay through neglect. Fortunately, the Reverend John Prince, author of the book, *Worthies of Devon* was vicar of the nearby church for 40 years, and it is to him we owe a debt of great magnitude for his descriptions of Berry Pomeroy castle in its heyday.

The Seymours, despite their wealth, seem to have over-reached themselves. Prince, writing in 1701, said that for all the money spent, it was never brought to completion. But the apartments within were magnificent, with alabaster statues and figures, costly marble chimneys, and so large that it was a day's work for a servant to open and close the casements. But the good vicar added: 'Notwithstanding which 'tis all demolished and all the glory lieth in the dust buried in its own ruins: there be nothing standing but a few broken walls which seem to mourn their own funerals. But what we may think strangest of all is that one and the same age saw the rise and fall of this noble structure.' The pity is that neither Prince, nor history, throws much light on why this splendid building was evacuated with such haste. Soon, verdurous festoons of ivy had claimed it.

Berry Pomeroy Castle, once seen, is never to be forgotten. The Seymours still take an interest in it and the splendid woodlands nearby, and the castle is looked after by the Environment Department.

How rich a place this is in its associations. Interwoven and entwined with the story of the Pomeroys and the Seymours is the history of Britain itself. Warriors of the conquering sword and Holy Cross and martyrs of other times are conjoined in this old pleasance. Pomeroys from Caen, Seymours from St Maur, Normandy; how many walked the ramparts, 100 feet long, from gatehouse to St Margaret's Tower, pondering their future and, perhaps, wondering on the pleasures and penalties of high birth. If there was a common bond between the families it was, perhaps, ambition and arrogance—and grievously they paid for it. The crowds, for example, on Tower Hill on 22 January, 1552, dipped pieces of cloth into the blood of felonious Somerset, owner of Berry Pomeroy, to keep as precious relics. Such are the chronicles of men and castles.

Tiverton

The funeral service of a Plantagenet Princess would have been a solemn, magnificent and unforgettable affair. And that of Catherine, daughter of King Edward IV of England, was no exception. She had lived at Tiverton Castle for 32 years, from 1495, when she married William Courtenay, himself from a line which produced a trio of Emperors.

'Her body, being embalmed, leaded and chested, was conveyed thence to the chapel, and placed within a box covered with black velvet on which was a cross of white satin.

'Upon that was another pall of cloth of gold, with a cross of silver tissue thereon, ornamented with the six escutcheons of her arms.

'There, it was attended with great pomp, when it lay in state 'til Monday 2nd December when, with a funeral service, it was brought to St Peter's Church. The Lord Suffragan, with all the other abbots and prelates in their pontificals, having performed the office of burial, went into the castle, where they had splendid entertainment.'

Dunsford's *History of Tiverton* tells all we need to know of the requiem of this august lady who had been contracted to marry the Spanish heir, and upon whose seal she was justified in describing herself as 'aunt, sister and daughter of kings'.

Her father, the licentious Edward IV, had made the mistake during his reign of setting up his wife's relations—the Greys and Woodvilles, as parvenu nobles. Perhaps the greatest event of his reign had been the establishment, under his patronage, of Caxton's printing press at Westminster. But when Catherine's brother, Edward, came to the throne as a boy, he was easy meat for the duplitious Gloucester who arranged the murder of the Princes in the Tower, and settled upon the throne himself. By so doing, he simply opened the way for the advent of the Tudor dynasty.

Tiverton Castle '... this great survival from the past—this historic stone shrine.'

Catherine was living at Tiverton Castle; a castle founded, it is said, on the orders of one of her ancestors, Richard de Redvers, Earl of Devon. Henry I had troubled dreams that the three estates of the realm, Lords, Church and Commons might unite against him, and ordered de Redvers—whom we shall meet again in the story of Devon's castles—to construct a stronghold above the River Exe, at Tiverton, and to defend it thereafter.

Following the King's instructions, the castle was completed in 1106. The de Redvers continued to hold the castle and the earldom until the direct male line became extinct in 1262. On the death of Avelina, daughter of the formidable Isabella, Countess of Devon in her own right, in 1293, the inheritance passed to her kinsman, Hugh de Courtenay, son of Reginald de Courtenay whom we have already met at Okehampton Castle. By 1335, Hugh had been created Earl of Devon. Tiverton Castle was their demesne for 260 years and, had

65

not William Courtenay married the Princess Catherine in 1495, they might be there to this day.

Nothing, it seemed, could halt the Courtenay climb. William and Catherine's son, Henry, was actually appointed heir-apparent by his cousin, the then childless King Henry VIII. The way to the English crown seemed open, as the King divorced one Queen after another in the attempt to produce a legitimate male heir.

Tiverton Castle was all pomp and circumstance, but in 1539, as we have seen, Henry Courtenay lost his head and with it all his family's hope for glory: even his son Edward, given a second glorious opportunity to succeed where his father had failed, spoiled his chances. On Henry Courtenay's death, the castle at Tiverton and the earldom passed to the Duke of Somerset. For a brief moment, under Bloody Mary, the estate and title reverted to Edward, but with his exile, and death in Padua, the Courtenay star faded from the heavens.

By the year of the Armada, Tiverton Castle had passed to Roger Giffard—a man who married three wealthy widows in rapid succession, and found the cash, thereby, to rebuild part of the castle. In the Civil War, the Roundhead General Fairfax put paid to the Giffards—as he did with the Carews at nearby Bickleigh Castle—and to the castle itself as a military stronghold, by demolishing the western fortifications.

The stone was used by its next owner, Peter West, a prosperous wool merchant, to create a Renaissance-style wing, but by 1727, the ever-hovering, hawk-like Carews moved in when Sir Thomas of that name married West's daughter, Dorothy.

For two centuries it was a Carew home until, in 1906, it was sold off. By 1960, Mr and Mrs Ivar Campbell, local landowners, moved in, and during their occupancy restored much of this lovely castle's grace and dignity. They shared such delight in their possession, and it was my privilege, as part of the Fourth Estate of the realm—how we laughed at Henry I's nightmares over the other three when we met—to write of their growing concern at the unsightly development in Tiverton which then threatened the environment of their beloved castle. Our laughter, I recall, was the more merry since the Campbells could trace their descent to King Henry I through the Plantagenets.

Their interests were wide, from clocks, a wonderful collection, of international repute, housed in the delightful south-east tower, to animals—a chapel of St Francis of Assisi was created at Tiverton Castle in 1971.

What is so immediately apparent in the ruins of the castle in the fine gardens is the immense depth of the walls. It is said, too, that there are secret passages between castle and the handsome church of St Peter's nearby. That may be pure conjecture. Once, it seems, this was a quadrangular castle with angle towers at each corner. Mighty it must have been in its heyday, though Fairfax, after an initial rebuff, seemed to have little enough difficulty in taking it from the Giffards.

Oddly, Tiverton Castle appears to have escaped the numerous fires which have beset the town itself. In 1598, for instance, and again in August, 1612, hundreds of houses were destroyed in Tiverton—the earlier as a result of a flash in a frying pan, the latter the result of the carelessness of an apprentice.

'No fyer from Heaven, such as worthily fell on the sinful cities of Sodom or Gomorrah matched that of the lamentable spoyle of Teverton,' wrote a contemporary, who witnessed both incidents, 'sodenly came that great grief upon them, which turned their wealth to miserable want, and their riches to unlooked for poverty; and how was that? Marry sir, by fyer!'

On a summer's evening, gazing west at the setting sun from Tiverton Castle, despite the insidious creeping of suburbia closer and closer to the castle walls, one might imagine that the whole sky was on fire at sunset beyond the western banks of the river below.

The Campbells have been succeeded at the castle by their kinsmen, the Gordons, who continue the monumental job of preserving for posterity this great survival from the past—this historic stone shrine.

Bickleigh

Long since, and in some quiet churchyard laid;
Some country nook, where o'er thy unknown grave
Tall grasses and white flowering nettles wave—
Under a dark-red-fruited yew-tree's shade.

Thus did Matthew Arnold write of *The Scholar Gipsy*, the academic who sought peace in pastoral surroundings.

The Carew family produced both a great scholar, in Richard, at Antony in Cornwall, and a gipsy, through Bampfylde at Bickleigh, in east Devon. Though their lives were separated by a century in time, their family name, Carew, lives on, through the immortal Survey of Cornwall of the one, and the eccentric and abandoned life-style of the other.

It is to Bickleigh Castle, past which the River Exe merrily flows on its journey towards Powderham, and the sea, that we must come if we would know more about the gipsy. This is the lovely middle valley of the River, far from the flat water meadows of the Exe delta. Rounded green hills rise on either side of Bickleigh Castle, which was used by the Courtenays when they owned it as the portion, or estate, for younger sons.

Here they consolidated the earlier Norman settlement until one of the Courtenay sons living here died, leaving an orphan daughter, Elizabeth. The Courtenays invited their cousins, the Carews, to look after the girl. She fell in love and eloped with Thomas Carew, to the anger of her family. But Thomas distinguished himself at the battle of Flodden (1513) where he is said to have saved the life of Lord Howard, the commander-in-chief. The Courtenays were so pleased

Right: The present owners of Bickleigh, Noel and Norma Boxall.

Ornamental gates at Bickleigh with the great gatehouse beyond.

that they gave Bickleigh Castle to Elizabeth as a delayed wedding present. The Carews continued the consolidation of this old castle and, with their Cornish cousins, made their mark on the history of the sixteenth and seventeenth centuries.

The castle's mighty gatehouse of pink sandstone seems to incorporate something of the three styles of architecture to be seen at Bickleigh Castle—Norman, medieval and Stuart.

Among the many interesting objects to be found here is the *Mary Rose* display, for, when that flagship of Henry VIII's fighting fleet disastrously keeled over in port, with its gunports open, and hundreds of English sailors were drowned, its commander, Vice-Admiral Sir George Carew, perished with the ship and his men. How the family must have grieved his passing, privately, perhaps, in the wonderful little chapel, created, it is believed, between 1090 and 1110. It was old when the Carew monuments of the sixteenth and seventeenth centuries were installed, and has survived to this day—the oldest, probably, in Devon.

Ironically, it was a Carew—not from Bickleigh—who sat in judgement on King Charles I—and paid with his head for regicide when the monarchy was restored—yet a Sir Henry Carew, a royalist, who held out at Bickleigh Castle against Fairfax. Cromwell's general had established camp at Cadbury, not far distant from Bickleigh, and 'slighted' it—destroying the fortified wings on the west and north side of the courtyard. Even the great gatehouse was damaged, but miraculously, the chapel escaped demolition.

Sir Henry Carew lived on until 1681 and died, it is said, broken-hearted, leaving no male heir to succeed owing to the tragic deaths, on the same day, of both his son and nephew at the tender ages of eleven and thirteen respectively.

Which leads us on to Bampfylde Moore Carew, born with the proverbial silver spoon in his mouth, but destined to become one of England's most famous vagabonds. Bampfylde, a good West-country name, sent by his father, the parish rector, to Blundells School at Tiverton, was wild and uncontrollable, and melted away with a band of Romanies, whom he had met in an alehouse regaling themselves on a feast of fowl, duck and other dainty dishes.

After eighteen months, the young man returned home to Bickleigh and was given a reception which would have pleased the Prodigal Son. But the taste of freedom proved irresistible, and before long Bampfylde was off again, living by his wits and aided by his extraordinary ability to impersonate other characters—from shipwrecked sailors to sorrowful clergymen.

This prince among confidence tricksters eventually succeeded Claude Patch as King of the Gipsies, and became a legend in his own lifetime. Past reform, Bampfylde was eventually arrested and transported to Maryland, to be sold into slavery. But iron chains could not contain him, and, after a series of high adventures with Red Indians, he managed to find a way back to Bristol, where he conned the crew into believing that he was suffering from smallpox. His life was a non-stop roundelay of outrageous behaviour—he even followed the Young Pretender to Derby doubtless thinking that he might dupe Prince Charles Edward himself.

But it was at Bickleigh where he died in 1758 and is said to be buried in an unmarked grave in the little churchyard. 'That thou wert wander'd from the studious walls to learn strange arts, and join a gipsy tribe; and thou from earth are gone long since . . .' The wanderer had returned, finally.

Legends abound about this castle, which is scarcely surprising in view of its remote position. There is a persistent piece of folk-lore, which some old Devonians may recall, of buried treasure in these parts. Cadbury Castle, ancient prehistoric hill fort looms on one side of the valley—and Dolbury Hill across the Exe in Killerton Park on the other. 'If Cadbury Castle and Dolbury Height dolven were,' runs the baffling old riddle, 'All England might plough with a golden sheere.' Golden treasure which is supposed to be guarded by a dragon. It has a Wagnerian ring about it.

And, it is said, on a midsummer's night across Bickleigh Bridge, a Carew warrior in glistening armour rides out to find a foe—disadvantaged, however, since his head is supposed to be tucked neatly under his arm!

The yellow roses now bloom in the beautiful gardens of Bickleigh Castle. There are hedges of honey-suckle. The old moat has been transformed into cool and pleasant pools of water where pink and white water lilies and irises compose themselves. The turbulence of times past has long disappeared: this is now a gentle scene of lambent sunshine flickering through leafy trees and glowing upon old castle walls.

Much has been done here since 1922 when the Carew estate at Bickleigh was sold off—much of the castle remains having been used as a farmhouse; the chapel had been a cattle byre. First the Harpers began the restoration work during the 1920s, and their efforts were continued by the Hensons. Now it is the present owners, Noel and Norma Boxall who give this castle their undivided attention, with all the work and the worry which it involves. Around them they have created both a home and a fascinating collection of memorabilia, much of it related directly to the 900 or so years of the history and the architecture of Bickleigh Castle.

Compton

Sweet Compton. Within these stout walls the pioneers of the first Elizabethan era plotted and planned their forays into North America and conquest of the Spanish Main. Battlements, buttresses and handsome oriel windows form the grand external features of this fortified mansion created by the Gilbert family. From the 1340s until the present day, except for an historic pause between 1800 and 1930, they have lived here—and returned to restore it, lovingly, to its former grandeur before presenting it to The National Trust for its preservation for all time.

Built on low-lying ground, like Powderham Castle, Compton Castle reeks of antiquity, its glorious facade, like a noble brow, wrinkled with age. It is astonishing to suddenly come upon it tucked away down a network of narrow Devonshire lanes at Marldon, not far distant from Torbay. But its imperishable claim to greatness lies not so much inside this elegant canopy, as through the deeds of the men and women associated with it. For here, truly, was sown the golden seed-corn of British Imperial splendour.

Four knights, all born to Katherine Champernowne, blazed meteoric trails across the skies of the sixteenth century. By her first husband, Otho Gilbert of Greenway, on the River Dart, Katherine bore John, Humphrey, Adrian and Elizabeth; when Otho died in 1547, Katherine married Walter Raleigh of Fardel manor, near Ivybridge, and gave birth to another Walter and Carew. Four sons were knighted—Sir John Gilbert, who succeeded to Compton Castle on his father's death, Sir Humphrey Gilbert, Sir Carew Raleigh and the incomparable Sir Walter Raleigh. They were super-stars in the Elizabethan establishment overshadowed only by the sun itself, the Queen. Bold, stern, sometimes arrogant men, they melted into amorous and ardent cupids before the might of their monarch.

Sir Humphrey Gilbert epitomised the spirit of the age, serving his

73

Above: In an English castle's garden—Compton. Right: Geoffrey Gilbert with his children Arabella, Humphrey and Walter—taken by his wife, Angela.

country with sword and pen. He set sail from Dartmouth in 1578 to colonize the West—America. The smallest in his fleet of seven ships was the little bark, the Squirrel. To this day, squirrels abound around Compton Castle. By extraordinary co-incidence, on the day I visited, a bushy-tailed grey squirrel, eyes bright with excitement, bounded in through the open Chapel door, and posed with its tiny front paws on the rim of a squirrel bowl.

But Sir Humphrey's first venture was unsuccessful. His fleet was forced back and, not until 1583 did he set forth again this time with five ships and 260 men. He reached Newfoundland. With only two ships surviving, he was obliged to set sail for home again. It was at midnight on 9 September that the little *Squirrel* foundered in the waves, sinking from the sight of its companion crew in the *Golden Hinde*. When last seen, the commander, Sir Humphrey, was observed at the ship's stern, reading a book. He hailed his

A friendly squirrel near a rare squirrel bowl in Compton Castle's chapel.

companions as the storm grew worse: 'We are as near to heaven by sea as by land,' were his words of encouragement.

The Elizabethans mourned his loss, summed up best, perhaps, in the lovely lyric from the pen of John Dowland, 'Now, oh now, I needs must part.' Years later, Winston Churchill was to write of the incident that 'the first great English pioneer of the West had gone to his death.' Gilbert's great venture had signalled the birth of an Empire.

But Humphrey's brother, Adrian, spurred on by heroic example and not diminished by tragedy, took on the task, with the determined help of his half-brother, Sir Walter Raleigh. It was Raleigh who, in 1584, despatched an expedition led by Sir Richard Grenville, which explored the area around Roanoke Island, which marked the birth of English-speaking America, 35 years before the Pilgrim Fathers set a foot on Plymouth Rock.

The Gilberts continued to feature in the annals of English

history—the seventh in line of descent from Sir Humphrey, Sir Walter Raleigh Gilbert (1785-1853) led a distinguished military career in India. Poised high above the Cornish town of Bodmin, to this day, is a 150-feet-tall obelisk commemorating his memory.

But it began in the country-scents of Compton Castle where the pears still ripen against warm cob walls. Old trees, older ruins and olden silence. Home of the pioneers in the tangled path of discovery.

From their painted portraits, now centuries old, we are given a glimpse of these men. Sir Humphrey, sallow and dark in appearance, much like a Spaniard, and so unlike his compatriot, the fresh-cheeked and ruddy-complexioned Sir Francis Drake. Raleigh, restless in nature, with the fingers of an artist, a great Englishman for all the defects of personality.

From the correspondence, we may discern the rich mosaic of their times. A letter from Sir John Gilbert to William Cecil with instructions for the care of a parrot given to Queen Elizabeth: '. . . he must be kept very warm, and after he hath filled himself (with meat) he will set in a gentleman's ruff all day. In the afternoon he will eat bread or oatmeal groats, drink water or claret wine . . . if he be taught well, he will speak anything.' We may only wonder how the Queen received this gift from the Gilberts.

Thanks to the late Commander Walter Raleigh Gilbert who gave Compton Castle to the National Trust in 1951, and stayed on, with his wife, to supervise much of the reconstruction and restoration, the house lives on. The Commander died in 1977: Mrs Gilbert retired from Compton in 1984 after 50 years in residence, and their son, Geoffrey Edmund Gilbert and his wife, Angela, and their children, Humphrey, Arabella and Walter Raleigh now occupy the family seat.

'A fine seat, set upon a knap of ground, environed with higher hills about it: whereby the heat of the sun is pent in, and the wind gathereth as in troughs . . .' The Elizabethan essayist, Francis Bacon may have had his reservations about such houses as that situated in this Devon valley at Compton, but even he had to admit that it produced great diversity—of both weather and men.

Plympton

Few, if any, of Devon's castles epitomise so exquisitely as does Plympton Castle the adaptability of the English people. The great truncated cone of earth was thrown up here before William the Conqueror crossed the Channel, making it a relatively light task for his supporter, Richard de Redvers, to create a round, stone shell, with walls eight feet thick and 30 feet high, radiating, like a beacon, the power of the Normans to all and sundry.

The people of Plympton, a busy and prosperous community long before even Plymouth had emerged, were cowed. Worse was to come when Richard's son, Baldwin de Redvers, defied King Stephen, and battled on Matilda's behalf at Exeter. While Baldwin was a good day's march away, Stephen sent in a powerful force of 200 horsemen and a body of archers and Plympton Castle, the focus of the nobleman's puissance, was partly razed to the ground—an act of revenge.

It was never rebuilt. Castles have invariably suffered more down the centuries than cathedrals in this respect. It has been said that if the cathedral is the apotheosis of architecture then the castle is architecture fighting for its life.

De Redvers had constructed the typical and traditional style of Norman castle at Plympton, which, in outline, resembles a keyhole. Motte (or mound) with shell keep on top (round in this instance) and a large, but well-contained bailey beneath the walls where, in Plympton's case, the lord would have established his residence. The castle keep at Plympton was never roofed over: it served the purpose of striking terror in the hearts of those who saw it. As an

Right: 'Plympton Castle has gazed out from its old mound for nigh on 900 years . . .'

early chronicler wrote of such establishments: 'The moles that the kepe stondeth on is large and of a terrible higth.'

Plympton, we must remember, was accessible from the sea at the time the castle was built. The Black Prince came up by boat when he visited the priory in the fourteenth century. And the ditch from which the material for the motte was dug made a perfect moat. Up to 200 years ago, the moat still existed and contained carp, among other fish. The castle moat also provided the site for a ducking-stool in which scolds were punished. Today, that moat has disappeared. By 1539, Plympton Castle was being described as utterly decayed, but just over a century later we learn that Prince Maurice occupied the bailey buildings with a very large force including five regiment of horse and nine of foot in the siege of Plymouth. The Royalists, however, evaporated, as the Roundheads marched to Plymouth's rescue. The bailey buildings suffered the same fate as the castle had done, centuries earlier.

But the people of Plympton had evidently grown attached to their castle, its moat and bailey. No longer did it offer a threat and, as we shall see, they began to adapt it for their own purposes. The bailey— or castle green—became a community centre, with all manner of old English 'sports' being enjoyed there, from bull-baiting and cock-fighting to wrestling and fairs. And what had been a Redvers-Courtenay stronghold became the property of the Earls of Morley, of nearby Saltram.

Early in the nineteenth century, the lord of the manor, Lord Boringdon attempted to assert his rights by sending his steward and a plough and pair of horses to the castle grounds. They met with fierce resistance. The Mayor and citizens captured the plough and made a bonfire of it. But the Morleys too had grown fond of the castle and its bailey and, in 1893, the Earl started a repair fund, and leased the property to the Plympton St Maurice Parish Council.

Victoria's Diamond Jubilee was celebrated there in style and, in 1922, there was another public demonstration at Plympton—this time of an entirely peaceful nature—to celebrate the transfer of the ancient castle to the parishioners.

The events of that September afternoon may be recalled from the programme. The church bells chimed, the band paraded and the council assembled outside the castle gate. The castle grounds were 'beaten', led by a Furry Dance, but it was the content of the Pageant of Plympton those many years ago which best reveals local beliefs about the castle. According to the producers of that pageant it was the ancient tribe of 'Damnonii' who first discovered the site and who threw up the earthworks. Druids, Romans and early Christians are associated with the site, long before King Stephen's troops stormed the keep.

But if these are long-forgotten associations, then that with Sir Joshua Reynolds is much more close and real, and a reminder that many celebrated visitors could not have failed to notice Plympton Castle, whose high and handsome motte and ruined shell keep was not shrouded in trees, as it is today.

John Wesley, King George III, Fanny Burney (the writer) and Sarah Siddons (the actress) and, inevitably in Joshua Reynolds's time, Samuel Johnson and James Boswell, not to mention, of course, in much earlier days, Plympton's great champion, Richard Strode, about whom we learnt more in the chapter on Lydford Castle, would all have been familiar with this ancient monument.

Plympton Castle has gazed out from its old mound for nigh on 900 years, witness to the changing face and fashions of time. It stood there in 1626, when the plague carried off one in five of the population hereabouts, and the superstitious whispered that the cause of the dread sickness was the conjunction of the planets Jupiter and Saturn. It was there too, rugged in its ruined strength, in 1967, when old Plympton was swallowed up by neighbouring Plymouth in the local government re-organisation.

And, perhaps, it is not too much to hope that it will still be there for centuries to come, a battered survival from the past recalling, for as long as it stands, the 'Honour' of Plympton, one of the greatest of all the feudal holdings in Devon extending all over the south west corner of the county. For, in those days, Plympton was the chief town, and Plymouth was no more than a small fishing village.

Plymouth

It is a mere scrap of history—but to the city of Plymouth it surely represents fidelity in stone. The calcicoles—the lime-loving wild flowers—flourish on and around this semi-circular tower. It is known as Castle Quadrate, and is to be found at the bottom of Lambhay Hill, on the Barbican.

Once upon a time, if we accept the accuracy of the ancient map makers, the burgeoning port of Plymouth boasted a small gate-house, flanked by turrets, at the water's edge, with steps leading up to a larger gatehouse defended by thick-flanking and embattled walls. The Barbican itself, Plymouth's old quarter, took its name from this defensive network.

The itinerant writer, Leland, saw it in 1535, and wrote: 'On the south side of this mouth is a Blok House and on a Rocky Hille hard by is a stronge Castel Quadrante, having at eche corner a great Roundtower. It semith to be no very old Peace of Worke.' But precisely what Leland meant by the observation in his final sentence has only served to puzzle the historians and archaeologists.

The defenders of the nascent Plymouth had earned themselves a reputation among would-be foreign invaders for their prowess and accuracy at stone-slinging. It is not too difficult to imagine, even today, that anyone armed with large chunks of rock on these cliffs of limestone above Sutton Harbour near Castle Quadrate would create mayhem among the crew of any ship attempting to make landfall.

It is evident that Plymouth had a castle—and the city stone-slingers would have made full use of its walls—but when, precisely, was it built? Opinion has been fairly divided—but many now tend to believe that the earlier date, of around 1220 to 1280 is probably correct, for all that Leland wrote in 1535. Sadly, much of the evidence has been destroyed. When the old castle became redun-

The final remnant of what was the south port of Plymouth Castle.

dant, a quarry was opened on the site to mine the rich belt of limestone. Most of the castle's foundations were swallowed up in the process, leaving us with only the venerable fragment, the Castle Quadrate.

'Here,' says the little plaque on its stout semi-circular wall, 'is the eastern part of the south port, the last remnant of the castle quadrant of Plymouth.' The quadrate is thought to be one of a pair of such towers which flanked the entrance to Plymouth Castle. It may never be possible to be more accurate than that.

In the late 1950s, when the Corporation decided to develop the area for much-needed housing, archaeologists were quick to take advantage of a once-in-a-lifetime opportunity of exploring the foundations. Their finds were interesting, but not as conclusive as many hoped. Where the quarry had been filled in, they discovered, a treasure-trove of seventeenth century objects, mainly of pottery and coins.

Castle Quadrant, Plymouth.

As the race went on with the builders, a defensive dyke some twenty feet wide at the top, fourteen feet wide at the bottom, and ten feet deep—and cut from solid rock, running east-west, was discovered. It helped confirm the existence of fortification on the site, but provided few clues for the purpose of dating the structure. The dyke was subsequently filled in.

The origins of Castle Quadrate must, therefore, remain something of a mystery, to be solved, perhaps, never at all or when advances in archaeology make it an even more precise science. Rigidly this small tower persists, awaiting an interpreter—defying time, an attitude in stone, the final blazon of a castle which helped nurture an infant city.

Watermouth

Just as Drogo is Devon's twentieth century castle, so Watermouth is the county's nineteenth century equivalent. Surprisingly few people are aware of it, however—and even Westcountrymen are baffled as to its location.

There could hardly be a better approach to Watermouth Castle than along the road which its owners created from Ilfracombe—an electrifying ride, or better still, walk—through some of the noblest and grandest coastal scenery to be found anywhere in Devon.

The castle lies close to a perfect small harbour, which probably induced A. Davie Basset to build here in the 1820s. Basset, whose family claimed links—as did Drewe at Drogo—with the Conqueror's army, found slate and stone from the mine workings in nearby Northfield Wood, to the south-east of the castle, and constructed a gothic-style medieval mansion, which was begun in 1825.

The outlook is magnificent. The castle faces the Bristol Channel, to the north. To the east lies the glorious twin hills, the mini-Matterhorn of Little Hangman (716 feet) and the even mightier Great Hangman in the background (1043 feet).

Heaven only knows what Basset found on the site apart from a collection of tunnels—all part of the fortifications, it was thought, of the little harbour of Watermouth nearby. Little is known about them to this day, and that serves only to whet Westcountry appetites with thoughts of smuggling—but of drink and baccy, not of deadly modern-day drugs.

From the original porch of a Basset property at Umberleigh, Davie brought elaborately decorated stonework panels dating from 1525, and parked them in the sub-tropical gardens of his new home.

Arthur Norway, in a travelogue written earlier this century described Watermouth as a gem of a place. 'That grand and beautiful domain that lies among sweet woods low down by the shore of a

Watermouth Castle '. . . a place where modern-day visitors can enjoy themselves . . .'

rocky cove. There are few sights in Devon fairer than the intersection of the valleys just beyond the castle, a labyrinth of winding field paths under deep plantations and threading meadow-lands so rich and verdant that one hardly sees the pheasants paddling away through the lush grass.'

That idyllic picture served to re-inforce the guide written in the middle of Queen Victoria's reign, 'A gothic building, unfinished, but commenced about 40 years ago by the father of the present pro-prietor. The situation is romantic, and the grouping of the neighbouring knolls and ridges strikingly beautiful. The castle stands at the edge of a green basin, little raised above the sea, but screened from it by a natural embankment of rocks. The richest woods enclose this vale, and a stream runs sparkling through the grass.

'The beautiful spot is viewed to most advantage from the sea, as the feudal-looking mansion and its verdant pastures are thence seen in connection with the bleak coast of Exmoor and the rocks of Ilfracombe. The cove should be visited, for it is a wild and cavernous recess.'

It would be invidious to try to improve upon those earlier descriptions, for the scenery and surroundings still tend to overwhelm the existence in their midst of a substantial castle with all the outward appearance of a typical medieval-style fortress created by some powerful baron.

One Basset, however, appeared to be something of an oddity. Beatrix Potter, not given to the sinister in nature, visited Watermouth Castle with her parents in 1882. As Lois Lamplugh explains in her history of Ilfracombe (Phillimore 1984) the young Miss Potter noted of the castle that it was owned by a Mr Basset, who had a large estate here. 'He was rather queer, they say he did not live at the castle but at a little house further on. His horse ran away with him and broke his neck at the corner of a field.'

The Bassets of Watermouth achieved some fame with their Gigantic Vertical Wheels, constructed in timber felled from their large North Devon estate. The wheel erected by Walter William Basset in Vienna at the turn of the century is still in use there—but it was said to have cost him a fortune, which he could ill afford, for all the acres of land his ancestors were said to have owned.

Walter's wife Harriet Mary, was fond of bizarre pets, including a bear which came to a grizzly end in a bran tub, and an orange-coloured cat with orange-coloured teeth which terrified the house staff, since they were obliged to accept responsibility for the wretched animal's breakages. Harriet Mary's daughter, Edith Penn-Curzon, turned the castle into a convalescent home for officers between 1916 and 1919, and was awarded a CBE. Of the cat, nothing further was heard.

By 1946, the Bassets departed Watermouth Castle, and taxation crippled its next owners, Mr and Mrs Nathaniel Black. Finally, in 1977 the castle was acquired by Richard and Antje Haines and their family, who have created holiday apartments and opened the mansion up to the public in a way which its builder could never have foreseen.

It has become a place where modern-day visitors can enjoy themselves and be amused through a wide variety of exhibits designed to appeal to all age groups. Devon's Victorian castle is, ironically, perhaps, the least stuffy of them all.

Dartmouth and Kingswear

See you the ferny ride that steals
Into the oak-woods far?
O that was whence they hewed the keels
That rolled to Trafalgar.

Seldom has Dartmouth been at peace. Her sailors ranged the seas perpetually. Her castle, or should we say castles, have, to my mind, stood guard and sentinel to the very walls of England—a sure turret mounted on a slate ledge above our island's great moat—the sea. Yet, of course, lest we Westcountrymen burst with pride at such silvery cadences, we must recall those other words of Kipling: 'Lo, all our pomp of yesterday is one with Ninevah and Tyre!'

The story of Dartmouth Castle, and its companion at Kingswear on the opposite bank of this glorious estuary, has been beautifully related by the late B.H. St J. O'Neil, former chief inspector of Ancient Monuments, in the official guide. In 1147 and again in 1190, he tells us, the estuary was one of the harbours used for the assembly of the Crusaders' Fleet. And how picturesque and colourful their departure would have been, for they took with them not merely military might but also the castle engineers and architects into the desert wastes of Syria and Lebanon—to Ninevah and Tyre. To the siege of Calais in 1346, Dartmouth sent 31 vessels, a fleet exceeded only by that of Fowey, with 47 ships. And, like Fowey with its estuarial twin, Polruan, Dartmouth and Kingswear were to be linked by a chain strung over the harbour mouth and anchored in the castles.

Left: Dartmouth and Kingswear Castles face each other at the mouth of the Dart Estuary.

The ever-present threat came from the French, and at its most acute, around 1388, the townspeople of Dartmouth began to construct their fortalice, or small fortress, by the water's edge, for the defence of their town and visiting vessels. This was during the mayoralty of that noteworty man of Dartmouth, John Hawley. Geoffrey Chaucer had been sent down to Dartmouth in 1373 by Edward III to make inquiries into the seizure of a ship and cargo belonging to a Genoan, with whom the King wished to remain on friendly terms.

It would have been a fairly delicate mission, since Dartmouth seamen had already established a notorious reputation for piracy on the high seas. Chaucer almost certainly had cause to remember Hawley thus in his Canterbury Tales prologue—

A Schipman was there dwelling far by Weste;
For ought I wot he was of Dert-e-mouthe.

Hawley died in 1408, but lived long enough to become embroiled in the defence of the port against the avengers from across the Channel. The Breton knight, du Chatel, eager to 'extirpate the Dartmouth vipers' landed at Slapton, around the corner, in 1404, with 300 ships and 2,000 men. Hawley took him on at Blackpool, supported by the women of Dartmouth who, it is said, fought like wildcats. The French fled, and Hawley, who took upon himself the profitable task of organising the ransom arrangements, apologised to Henry IV for being unable to attend court because of a leg injury.

It was almost a century (in 1481) before Dartmouth obtained the castle which we know today. The strong square tower which juts out defiantly and commands the maritime approaches to the harbour. On the other side, Kingswear Castle was begun in 1491 and finished by 1502. Dartmouth Castle was built of strong Charleton slate, quarried from near the village poised between the two arms of the Kingsbridge Estuary. The site selected at Kingswear was near the ruins of an earlier structure, known as Godmerock.

The chain across the haven mouth was not a novelty even in the 1480s, but Dartmouth's military armaments were as modern as any in the kingdom. The eastern end of the chain, however, so Mr O'Neil tells us, was fastened to an unspecified point (Godmerock, perhaps?) on the rocks opposite Dartmouth Castle since Kingswear Castle was incapable of holding it. But the chain proved useful on at least two occasions—in 1599, against Spain, and in 1642 during the Civil War. After the Restoration in 1660, Dartmouth Castle became Crown property, as it still is. O'Neil tells us that its strength, in 1667, resulted in the Dutch fleet sailing by, without daring to attack. Above the castle itself is the Civil War redoubt known as Gallants Bower, and at Bayard's Cove are the not inconsiderable remains of defensive works created in 1537 as a part of Henry VIII's coastal defence scheme.

If Dartmouth throughout its long history has bristled with the impedimenta of war, then let us not overlook its role as the cockpit for adventures of other kinds. Their ships were, by modern standards, almost laughable in their frailty. Think of Adrian Gilbert of Compton Castle or John Davis of Sandridge, the latter putting to sea in two cockleshell-sized ships named, would you believe, *Sunneshine* and *Moonshine*.

Brave adventure. Setting forth from Dartmouth for the unknown white wastes, the perils of the polar pack, the search for the North-West passage and, most valiant of hearts, forever nursing and nurturing unconquerable hope. This was the port in which Richard Coeur de Lion's fleet gathered: where Chaucer quested and quizzed: from whence the strange and terrible William Rufus embarked for Normandy, and from where, in our own times, part of the mighty armada of salvation set sail to rescue all Europe from the yoke of a tyrannical maniac called Hitler.

Dartmouth Castle stands to this day—a monument well worth the visit: but see it from the sea if you can, or from a point above Kingswear Castle, now the home of Sir Frederick Bennett M.P.

To think, that Kingswear cost a mere £68 to build, and was described in 1717 as useless and irreparable.

I laugh not at an others loss,
I grudge not at an others gaine:
No worldly waves my mynde can toss,
My state at one dothe still remayne:
I feare no foe, I fawne no freende,
I lothe not lyfe, nor dread no ende.

ACKNOWLEDGMENTS

It has been a singular joy for me to work on this book with my two sons, Julian, who proved an admirable and thoughtful companion with his camera throughout our travels, and his younger brother, Stephen, whose illustrations will, I hope, provide the reader with as much pleasure as they have given me.

I wish to thank, also, the courteous owners and curators of the castles with whom I came into contact, the Devon County archivist, Mrs M. Rowe, and the staff of the Plymouth City Library whose willingness to help seems inexhaustible. All errors and omissions are of my own making.

There are many books from which I have gleaned information written by authors whom, you will discover when you read them, share a common pleasure in the castles of Devon.

Some books are, sadly, no longer in print, but I would mention, in particular *Castles* by Charles Oman (GWR 1926); *The English Castle* by Hugh Braun (Batsford 1936); *Highways and Byways in Devon and Cornwall* by Arthur Norway (Macmillan 1930); *Murrays Handbook for Devon and Cornwall* (1859) reprinted by David and Charles 1971; *Dartmouth* by Ray Freeman (Harbour Books 1983); *Archaeology of the Devon Landscape* (DCC 1980); *A History of Devon* by Robin Stanes (Phillimore 1986); *Devon* by W.G. Hoskins (1954); *Reflections on the Puritan Revolution* by A.L. Rowse (Methuen 1986); *The Buildings of England* by Nikolaus Pevsner (Penguin 1952); *Motoring and Seeing Castles in Devon* by A.L. Clamp (Westway Guides 1967); the *Transactions of the Devonshire Association* (various); *A Perambulation of Dartmoor* by Samuel Rowe (Devon Books 1986); *Walking Dartmoor's Ancient Tracks* by Eric Hemery (Hale 1986); *Powderham* by Lady Paulina Pepys (English Life Publications); *Archaeological Sites of Devon and Cornwall* by Tom Clare (1982); *High Dartmoor* by Eric Hemery

(Hale 1983); *Gems in a Granite Setting* by William Crossing (reprint Devon Books 1986); *Historic Dart* by Eric Hemery (David and Charles 1982); *Portrait of Dartmoor* by Vian Smith (Hale, 1966); *Barnstaple* by Lois Lamplugh (Phillimore 1983); *Proceedings of the Plymouth Athenaeum* Vol V *Plympton St Maurice* by Audrey Mills; *Two Thousand Years in Exeter* by W.G. Hoskins together with numerous guide book accounts of individual castles (H.M.S.O. and The National Trust) and newspaper cuttings from The Western Morning News.

ALSO AVAILABLE

DARTMOOR IN THE OLD DAYS
by James Mildren
James Mildren is an author who is at home in the wilderness of his Dartmoor.
'Lovers of Dartmoor will need no persuasion to obtain a copy. To anybody else, I suggest they give it a try. It may lead to a better understanding of why many people want Dartmoor to remain a wonderful wilderness.'
Keith Whitford, The Western

HISTORIC INNS OF DEVON
by Monica Wyatt
The author visits 50 famous hostelries scattered over the county.
'Monica Wyatt's writing is pitched at just the right level . . . thoroughly researched, shot through with real enthusiasm and never donnish. She shares her discoveries with you . . . I raise my glass.'
The Western Evening Herald

PEOPLE AND PLACES IN DEVON
by Monica Wyatt
Dame Agatha Christie, Sir Francis Chichester, Dr David Owen, Prince Charles and others. Monica Wyatt writes about eleven famous people who have contributed richly to the Devon scene.
'A very interesting title for this rapidly expanding publishing house, indeed for a "cottage" industry its going from strength to strength, its territory now covering an area from Bristol to Land's End.'
Irene Roberts, The South Hams Newspapers

MYSTERIES IN THE DEVON LANDSCAPE
by Hilary Wreford and Michael Williams
Outstanding photographs and illuminating text about eerie aspects of Devon. Seen on TSW and Channel 4. Author interviews on DevonAir and BBC Radio Devon.
' . . . reveals that Devon has more than its fair share of legends and deep folklore.'
Derek Henderson, North Devon Journal-Herald

AROUND GLORIOUS DEVON
by David Young
David Young, well-known in the Westcountry as TSW's roving architect, takes us on a personally-conducted tour of his glorious Devon.
' . . . proves as good a guide in print as he is on the small screen.'
Judy Diss, Herald Express

94

SEA STORIES OF DEVON

In this companion volume to *Sea Stories of Cornwall* nine Westcountry authors recall stirring events and people from Devon's sea past. Well illustrated with old and new photographs, it is introduced by best-selling novelist, E.V. Thompson.
'The tales themselves are interesting and varied, but the real strength of the book lies in the wealth of illustration, with photographs and pictures on practically every page.'

Jane Leigh, Express and Echo

GHOSTS OF DEVON

by Peter Underwood

Peter Underwood, President of the Ghost Club, writes of the ghostly stories that saturate the county of Devon, a land full of mystery and of ghostly lore and legend.'
'Packed with photographs, this is a fascinating book.'

Herald Express

LEGENDS OF DEVON

by Sally Jones

Devon is a mine of folklore and myth. Here is a journey through legendary Devon, Sally Jones brings in to focus some fascinating tales, showing us that the line dividing fact and legend is an intriguing one.
'Sally Jones has trodden the path of legendary Devon well . . .'

Tavistock Times

DARTMOOR PRISON

by Rufus Endle

A vivid portrait of the famous prison on the moor stretching from 1808—with rare photographs taken inside today.
'The bleak Devon cage's 170 year history . . . fascinatingly sketched by one of the Westcountry's best known journalists Rufus Endle . . . the man with the key to Dartmoor.'

Western Daily Press

STRANGE STORIES FROM DEVON

by Rosemary Ann Lauder and Michael Williams

Strange shapes and places—strange characters—the man they couldn't hang, and a Salcombe mystery, the Lynmouth disaster and a mysterious house are only some of the strange stories.
'A riveting read.'

The Plymouth Times

95

OTHER BOSSINEY TITLES:

CASTLES OF CORNWALL
by Mary and Hal Price

HEALING, HARMONY AND HEALTH
by Barney Camfield

LOVING, LAUGHING AND LIVING
by Barney Camfield

WESTCOUNTRY HAUNTINGS
by Peter Underwood

OCCULT IN THE WEST
by Michael Williams

WESTCOUNTRY MYSTERIES
Introduced by Colin Wilson

PARANORMAL IN THE WESTCOUNTRY
by Michael Williams

SECRET WESTCOUNTRY
by Rosemary Clinch, Hilary Wreford and Michael Williams

We shall be pleased to send you our catalogue giving full details of our growing list of titles for Devon, Cornwall and Somerset and forthcoming publications.

If you have difficulty in obtaining titles, write direct to Bossiney Books, Land's End, St Teath, Bodmin, Cornwall.